To Lausie
Happy 17th Birthday
With love Grandd

Peter Megargee Brown

Memories enrich our lives.
Recall the best —
and write them down.
—— ——

FLIGHTS
Of Memory
DAYS
Before Yesterday

FLIGHTS
Of Memory
DAYS
Before Yesterday

PETER MEGARGEE BROWN

A Memoir

BENCHMARK PRESS

Published by:

BENCHMARK PRESS

100 Park Avenue, Suite 2606
New York, New York 10017

Library of Congress Cataloging-in-Publication Data

Brown, Peter Megargee

Flights of Memory: Days Before Yesterday—A Memoir/
Peter Megargee Brown—First Edition

ISBN 0-915011-034

1. Memories—New York City, Carnegie Hill; Bermuda; Greek Mediterranean, Philadelphia.
2. 1929 Crash and Big Depression—Crash of 1987.
3. Pleasures of reading and writing it down.
4. Teachers and Mentors.
5. Time and Wisdom.
6. Power of Remembrance.

Library of Congress catalogue #89-60659
Some of the chapters have been published, in
slightly altered form, in *The Bermudian* magazine.

Manufactured in the United States of America
Produced by Fred Weidner & Son, Printers, Inc.
The book set in Electra by Partners Composition
Printed and Bound by Penmor Lithographers
Jacket and book design by DANIEL J. McCLAIN
First Edition
10 9 8 7 6 5 4 3 2 1

CONTENTS

TO MY MOTHER MIRIAM
*who taught me about
the fun of life and love*

AUTHOR'S PROLOGUE

Our Personal Memory System

PEOPLE IN ALL PARTS of the world enjoy looking back to earlier days. This is not a curse of unbridled nostalgia. Reflections can be a healthy and inexpensive way to derive pleasure and meaning from our past experiences.

This exciting curiosity has existed since at least the beginning of recorded time. The poet Homer recited from memory (his and others) the glorious deeds and dreadful perils of Aegean life in masterful stories of *The Iliad* and *The Odyssey*. In a young upwardly mobile country such as America, we are sometimes reluctant to admit that we too relish a glance backwards, particularly if the look encompasses our original community, our own people and, most of all, our own family.

The human mind is primarily constructed to view and deal with the present. Some of us have the special gift of envisioning the future—what we call possessing psychic vision. The present is logically part of the future and inevitably becomes a part of the past.

Our human minds, I believe, are still the best computers, better than any others on today's market. Psychiatrists tell us we use only a fraction of our capacity to review the past through the hindsight of memory and to foresee the future based on our insights and our crucial experience.

This book is about using our given mental potential to retrieve more efficiently and more happily the memory tapes inside us, in order to replay them on command for enjoyment and enrichment of our lives.

Psychologist William James, brother of novelist Henry James, recognized that the one who "thinks over his experiences most and weaves them into systematic relations with each other will be the one with the best memory."

There are some memories, painful, neurotic or banal, we would prefer to erase—to forget. With discipline, we can learn to boycott unpleasant films of memory and bring forth, at will, the best of our earlier experiences. We can learn to recall not only exciting challenging events, first experiences, but also poignant and loving relationships with others, some family, some not, but all intimacies that stick with us as the true substance of our lives.

I began to play the memory game in the Army when I was a private in the infantry for two years in World War II. By using your innate memory system you can develop, on the spot, a relief from the brain-dead horror of boredom and oppression. All of us have in our past moments of joy, of love, of heroic events. Sacrifice, exhilaration of success, consummation, redemption and the grace of forgiveness. The scripts are as broad in spectrum as life is itself.

Scientists have recently discovered that when we become more mature (aging is not a subject of this book) we begin to experience a *greater* facility to recall—sometimes in startling detail—events, places, people, conversations, colors, smells and narrative that we thought had long ago been buried in the past. This phenomenon has been recently labelled "episodic memory." This book is episodic memory for the most part and could not have been written without it. Our memory system is a truly democratic gift. We all can, with a little conscious effort and a proper introduction, learn to utilize this gift without fear of going bankrupt or incurring the wrath of the Surgeon General. And when we travel we can take it with us, fueling our memory-recall system on our trip with the songs of our own experiences.

Cicero, as early as 80 B.C., reminds us that memory is the "treasury and guardian of all things."

Of course much of our memories stored away in the banks of our mind will be subjective. Naturally much of our memory will relate to family relationships. This circumstance often leads to sifting through our family connections, going back in generations as far as memory can take us. These recollections are fostered by research, by more elderly family members of keen recollection, such as grandmothers, and sometimes by studying our cache of family treasures like Bibles or scrolls or ancient letters, even postcards, telling us poignant bits and pieces of our past on this earth.

To suggest a retrospection touching on family would have been embarrassing some years ago. But in 1976 Doubleday published a widely acclaimed book by Alex Haley called *Roots*. It was followed by a triumphal Brandon Stoddard television series that gripped the attention and conscience of America and beyond. Since then an enormous portion of live human beings have been sparked to look to the past to see where they came from and to use and obtain from others the memories of early days. So from then on many Americans have seemed more comfortable with glancing back to earlier days, no matter what the past struggles might have entailed.

Alex Haley's grandmother, you may recall, used to tell him stories about their family—stories going back to *her* grandparents and their grandparents, "down through the generations all the way to a man she called 'the African.' " The author spent a dozen years, travelling a half-million miles across three continents searching for documentation. Finally, Alex Haley identified his ancestor—Kunta Kinte—and also the location of the village in the Gambia, West Africa, from which he was abducted in 1767 at sixteen years of age and kidnapped on the ship Lord Ligonier to Maryland and there sold to a Virginia planter. What a story, what a quest and what a grand feast for the memory system of Kunta Kinte's descendants.

But remember that the great writer-thinker Chekhov strongly contended that "good stories" do not come straight from real experience but evolve from "contemplation of an essence of it."

Two years ago Katharine Hepburn published a fascinating book, out of her own memory bank, back 35 years ago, *The Making of THE AFRICAN QUEEN or How I Went to Africa with Bogart, Bacall and Huston and Almost Lost My Mind.* Her episodical recollection book, with a jaunty photograph of the great actress on the cover, tells, in delightful detail, what it was like for her in London and in Africa to meet John Huston, Humphrey Bogart and Lauren Bacall for the very first time, and to work with each of them constantly for three months under incredibly difficult, if humorous, circumstances.

Using her own memory-recall system with grand precision, Katharine Hepburn takes us with her on an extraordinary adventure, so charming, so immediate in her recollections, that we are transported there with her. She tells us she had fun and that special spirit is conveyed instantly to the reader. This is her first book, dedicated, simply, "To Mother and Dad."

How could Katharine Hepburn recall such stunning details after over thirty years? In the opening of her book she enlightens us by saying that while she has never written a diary, *"there are some happenings you can't forget.* There they are. A series of facts—pictures—realities. This happened to me with *The African Queen*. I remember it in minute detail—I can see every second of its making and of me at the time of—

"Well, I thought so many people have asked me— what was it like? And I got to jotting down bits here, bits there.

"And then I thought:

"Come on dear—pull it together.

"So here it is—thirty-odd years after the fact."

With the magical use of her own episodic memory system, in time inherent in all of us, Katharine Hepburn shows us the way and the sheer joy of it!

FOREWORD

I HAVE ENJOYED receiving love notes from Peter over the years. Now he's written down his first book of personal recollections. I was present at the creation as Peter wrote these intimate sketches and I saw sweat pour from his forehead—not so much in angst as from deep feelings of appreciation—as he painted happy scenes from his life he wanted to relive and share.

Daily conversations with Peter are stimulating and often inspiring, simply because Peter is a Renaissance man who makes his life with his family and as a lawyer a colorful daily adventure. Many of us know something of the public life of Peter Megargee Brown, and now we glimpse into his personal reminiscences, his loves and the fun of living.

I'm touched to have him share some painterly strokes with us of his private delights. This book is about contentment. Peter lives with delightful sensitivity. His essays give a glimpse of happy "days before yesterday." He makes us aware how much pleasure he derives from doubling his happiness by writing his memories. He lives, writes and loves these memories.

We all have "flights of memory." I hope Peter's book of essays makes you feel the exhilaration of his joy of living and you become inspired to write your own private remembrances. There are xerox machines and publishers and the message here is to live triumphantly and record these private thoughts of yourself, your family, your friends and above all, for all times.

ALEXANDRA STODDARD
January 9, 1989
New York City

–I–

SIXTY-ONE YEARS OVER THE RAILROAD TRACKS

Living in the City of Final Destination

I was brought to the top of Carnegie Hill, exactly 93rd Street and Park Avenue in New York City, 61 years ago. I was five years old and by exercise of what is now called "episodic memory," I can recall that first day quite well. It is a strange feeling to still live on Carnegie Hill for more than half a century and see the flickering changes along the avenue and side streets of this somewhat small town neighborhood. The staying-put stimulates remembrances of early days and slows the rush of turbulent modern times.

Over the years E. B. White reminded us that the man born somewhere else than in New York City who comes here "in quest of something" is the most fortunate for he has a "city of final destination, the city that is a goal."

Park Avenue just a few years before my modest arrival was an open eyesore sewer of uncovered railroad tracks from which Commodore Vanderbilt's locomotives belched soot and steam as the coal-fed trains rattled north and south through thick granite tunnels.

By 1927 the railroad tracks had been mercifully sunk and covered in a master plan of some constructive imagination.

Instead of shanties, pigsties, saloons and breweries strewn in muddy squalor, elegant verdant center-island malls and handsome townhouses sprang to life along the newly named "Park Avenue" from the new Grand Central Station to 96th Street.

The world of fashion was mesmerized by this sudden transformation from low-scale to upscale and the herd-like stampede began of masters, matrons and mistresses to Park Avenue from Fifth and Madison Avenues.

My father located and purchased, with my mother's dowry, cooperative apartment 9B at 1172 Park Avenue on the southwest corner of 93rd Street, across from financier George F. Baker's red brick Georgian mansion (now the cathedral of the Greek Orthodox Church).

My father kept insisting his selected location was the highest point of land in Manhattan—a point of pride, often repeated to guests who ventured "uptown." But the late United States Senator Jacob Javits denied this boast, instead claiming that where *he* was born in Washington Heights was higher. So be it. From early days my two sisters and brother would whoop and holler in the snowstorms, somehow more frequent in those days, choosing either south, north, east or west to slide down on our battered Rosebud Eagle sleds. To us, 93rd and Park was the apex— our world. A community around us all our own.

Each day the railroad hidden under Park Avenue brought in and out over 100,000 commuters from the outskirts of the city. Day and at night I heard the poignant sounds from the tracks below of the trains, now electrified, rattling, grinding and squeaking their sinuous sonorous way to and from Grand Central, two miles to the south. Today, I still live over the Park Avenue railroad tracks, just a few yards away, in constant earshot of the resonance of the railroad trains traveling to and fro. I don't regret one whit the indignity associated with my location over the railroad tracks, so downgraded in American literature, or constantly hearing the clackety-clack of the railroad cars. In fact, the railroad trains just below my window have become a kind of comfort, a companion of noise and thunder, as much a part of life as memory and family.

Not long ago, a familiar snowstorm brought me home early to my apartment on Carnegie Hill, high over the same railroad tracks. Delivered to my door that day was a brochure entitled, "The Park Avenue Railroad Tunnel: A Program of Restoration" distributed by Metro-North Commuter Railroad that for the past three years, I learned, has been surveying the awful condition of my subterranean railroad tunnel.

The brochure cover had a magnificent shot sweeping north along Park Avenue from the vantage of 90th Street, and the vintage of turn-of-the-century, showing the splendor of the partly covered tracks further down and the broad car-less, people-less boulevards and gaslight brownstones, dressed with breezy striped awnings. And one photograph, aiming south from 93rd Street, in modern times ending with the chopped-off Citicorp Center and the timeless art-deco Chrysler Building, where I worked one summer for $10 a week.

The photographs invoked unashamed nostalgia. The brochure noted seriously that the Park Avenue railroad tunnel had been built over the past 15 decades in a rather helter-skelter fashion, somewhat like a Disney catacomb. Work on restoration, the report advised, would commence shortly.

But certain extreme deterioration was found at—where else?—93rd and Park Avenue, which *could* bring on an "emergency" closing down of rail traffic entirely. Apparently Commodore Cornelius Vanderbilt, between 1872 and 1874, mined through solid granite at 93rd Street (26 feet below street level), a 596-foot short-cut tunnel which can only be repaired from underground. Water infiltrated portions of the brick lining of the 148-year-old tunnel. Subsequently, Metro stopped leaks, installed bolts and secured the brick lining with drains. Out of sight we can hear the Metro workmen doing their job in the dead of night.

I remember that first September day in 1927, refreshingly warm and smelling of hops, like the odor of burnt carrots, while crossing Park Avenue with the family newly arrived to the mysteries of the city. We had walked down 93rd Street to Madison Avenue by the Alamo apartments which in 1945 became the locus of the film "The House on 92nd Street"—actually on 93rd, and still is. Then a stroll to Central Park through the Engineers' Gate where signs placed by the Parks Department on the lawns of the green meadow said, inhospitably, "Keep off the Grass."

Upon this Olympian hill, there still remained some years ago two earnest, if flamboyant, German brewers providing the Yorkville area with honorable beer—George Ehret (see his old ad and logo at P. J. Clarke's ancient bar), and the venerable fur-coated Jacob Ruppert, who annually tossed out the first baseball at the Yankee Stadium (see annual picture in the disappeared *Daily Mirror*). Mr. Ehret built his mansion at 94th Street and Park Avenue where now is the large court-yarded 1185 Park Avenue. Mr. Ruppert's breweries lay to the East a few blocks from Park, its copper vats attended by German immigrants with cloth caps, their magnificent mustaches foaming with golden brew. In this odoriferous area I was first mugged at the corner of 91st and Madison by a young Irish lad who fled east, my brother in knickers in keen pursuit.

When the Metro survey pinpointed 93rd and Park Avenue as the crisis area, I wondered whether Wall Street tycoon George F. Baker had somehow contributed to the trouble by persuading the railroad to give him the privilege of a private spur under his own mansion at 93rd and Park Avenue.

This was surely the golden age of the railroad. The private cars of the financial barons were resplendent in style unmatched in comfort and grandeur today. Mr. Baker had followed the canny lead of Andrew Carnegie who between 1889 – 1903 (on squatter's territory with goats from Central Park) built his ultimate Georgian Mansion between 90th and 91st on Fifth Avenue. The wily Scot bought up the neighboring land and sold it to "suitable people." His great house is now the Cooper-Hewitt Museum. Carnegie also had his own private railroad car (a well-kept secret, if true) parked and perked under his resplendent quarters overlooking Central Park. A long way from his modest birth cottage at Perth, Scotland, high on a similar hillside overlooking the Perth river and two busy distilleries.

Across from Carnegie's mansion to the south was a temporary tennis court on Fifth Avenue. The afternoon after I arrived on the Hill in September 1927 (Charles A. Lindbergh had landed in Paris and made the first Man-of-the-Year cover of *Time Magazine*), my father, out of a mixture of kindness and frustration, took me on a walk through the neighborhood, now called by developers Carnegie Hill. He approached the tennis court at 90th Street where there was a large new sign which proclaimed: "On this Site will be built the Church of the Heavenly Rest (Episcopal)." My father pointed his cane at the sign. "See that," he said, raising his voice, "that's where *you* will be going to church—whether you like it or not." The church had purchased the valuable lot from Mrs. Carnegie for a million dollars on the condition that the roof would be low enough to allow her sufficient sun on her own garden to the north across 90th Street. The Heavenly Rest has no steeple.

Later that day my mother took me on one of her "errands"—to find little shops to feed a family of six. I remember going to Third Avenue and 89th Street where enormous *elevated* railroad trains roared by, deafening us for minutes afterward. Conversation would simply stop mid-sentence and resume unperturbed a few moments later. At that junction was a colorful fruit and vegetable stand (not unlike the Impressionist painting of a fruit stand by Caillebotte) manned by Mike with the coal black eyes. He polished and sold the best and we returned regularly to his stand under the El. He also sold, next door, both pink and white horseradish, freshly ground on the street by Mike, one hand grinding, one hand amiably touching his cap.

We passed a stationery store on the way home. The red sign said, "La Primadora." Mother stopped in to enter a daily subscription to *The Herald Tribune*, which at that time featured Beatrix Potter's Peter Rabbit. The owner of the shop, two steps down, was an ebullient and friendly man, known to us as Mr. Epstein. He relished the starting subscription and the new family entering the small neighborhood. He gave me as encouragement a penny chocolate.

When I returned one day to the Hill on a furlough from the Army in 1945, eighteen years later, I walked by his shop, now larger, on the other side of the street. There was a sign in the window written by hand in block letters: "This Shop is Closed Today," it said, "one-half in Memory of the death of Mr. Epstein and one-half in the Memory of the Death of our President, Franklin Delano Roosevelt."

In those days women did not work and were known as housewives except for those who were nurses, teachers or nuns. Being a housewife was no easy breeze as I recollect it. Mother was up at dawn and worked on a variety of scheduled chores until long after dark. She bought all the groceries, fish, meat and supplies herself in a round of little neighborhood stores whose merchants were glad for the business and gave anecdotal good cheer and service when we would enter their domains. I soon learned that an alert housewife could secure a cut of beef more tender and less costly if the proper relationship had been established with Joe the butcher. Joe wore a wide-brimmed straw hat, he said, so he would reduce colds in his head, running as he did, back and forth into his ice-cold refrigerator. He gained some notoriety in the neighborhood by asking Mrs. Wallman (who complained to him that his chicken did not smell good) whether she herself could pass such a test.

I liked these visits with my mother around the Hill, my brother George being at Browning School (where you could wear a smart cap with a brown "B" emblazoned on it) and my oldest sister, Harriett, at Mrs. Dickerman's Classes (called Todhunter) where the President's wife Eleanor taught the students current events in a precise and

7

melodious fashion and my other sister, Bebe, at Brearley School at old quarters on Park Avenue in the 60s. (My mother preferred Brearley after the headmistress of Miss Hewitt's Classes handed her *The Social Register* and inquired imperiously, "Tell me who you know, Mrs. Brown."

One evening in the early 1930's, my father called me into the library. He wanted to talk to me about an important event in my life. I was all curiosity for what could be his announcement? He said: "It's about time you went to school and I think you should start now." "Where?" I asked, hoping it would be Browning. "No, someday maybe, but now you're too young and your reading and writing is non-existent, don't you think?" (He liked to say aphorisms, as if to himself, like, "The infinite capacity of the human mind resists the introduction of knowledge.") He then got up and looked out the window across to the reservoir and the twin-towered building on the west side of the park. "I have talked today to the headmistress of Miss Caldwell's School and she is willing to take you now," he said, as if there would be no argument. I remember saying that I heard that Miss Caldwell's was a girl's school. "Yes," he said, "it is a girl's school, but Miss Caldwell tells me they have one boy currently enrolled this term. Be ready to go tomorrow after breakfast." And that was that. I was not in the mood for introduction of knowledge at a girl's school.

Miss Caldwell's for the next year was an experience hard to forget. Miss Caldwell did her daily disciplining of her students, mostly myself and the other boy, in her dark panelled front room on the second floor of the dank and gloomy brownstone, off Madison on 62nd Street. I remember she sat, an enormous blob of black dress, in a tattered wing chair. She had a grey mustache which she stroked with one hand while tapping a ruler on her thigh. She began her monologue with a fervid appeal to generational contrast. "After meeting your father and your mother, I cannot understand (repeat "cannot understand") how they could have a son so devoid (repeat "so devoid") of elementary good manners. You are constantly disrupting the decorum of my school. *And* Mr. Brown, I will not have it!" [slapping ruler on thigh]. Then she would end her diatribe by whispering, "Do you have anything to say?" I would reply something to the effect that I was sorry and it would not happen again.

One day a new teacher was assigned to our class (8 girls, 2 boys). Her name was Miss Perrin, young, warmspirited, a tad plump. We were all delighted to have her as our teacher for the rest of the year. She read fascinating stories to us and taught us to write sentences. I was a slow learner and she cheerfully persevered. When my mother and father went down to Bermuda at Eastertime that year on the Furness Line, Miss Perrin insisted I write my parents a letter, an obvious impossibility on my part. But I recall that Miss Perrin was eager to have her pupil do the letter properly and drew pencil lines across white paper, one line for capital letters and a lower line for regular letters. After I laboriously printed out the "How Are Yous" within her constraints, she magically erased the pencil lines leaving a missile to mother and father that did not look too bad. But the letter to them at the white-clapboarded Hamilton Princess hit like a stick of dynamite. "My God," my father exclaimed to my biased mother, "the kid can write a letter!" Miss Perrin still floats delightfully in my memory even to this day.

The trains below on Park Avenue are noisier now, not unpleasantly so, but more defined, as if orchestrating a melody of the 150 years of coming and going. I think about first arriving, hand held, at 93rd Street and Park and wondering what this neighborhood would bring to us next.

Then the sounds from the tracks come louder and louder—the click-click, the rumble, faster and faster, and then, as quickly, fading out, slowly, slowly, until there is no sound except automobiles licking the melting snow as they rise to make the big hill at 93rd and Park. Then I hear (I think for the first time) a mordant sound of a train's horn *whoooaaa*—strange. Something may be wrong on the railroad track under Park Avenue. Faint thunder now and a brisk rumble and cough as the night deepens. Trains on the old railroad track below me rush on to the suburbs and beyond, carrying away what E. B. White called commuters "devoured by locusts each day and spat at each night." When I think about it, I am more than satisfied with my own final destination right here over the railroad tracks—particularly during these past 61 years.

−II−

THAT FIRST BERMUDA SUMMER A HALF CENTURY AGO

I n the winter of 1937, my father announced to my mother and their four children, "This summer we're all going to Bermuda." Excitement was intense. We lived on a city of concrete, high on Carnegie Hill. The weather was cold in winter and, air conditionless, hot as hell in summer. We dreamed of the sentient pleasures awaiting us in just a few months. My father, an original organization man, made the plans. Down on the Monarch; back on the Queen. A small white cottage up Southcote road, in Paget, seven minutes by foot on the white coral road to the sea.

On the turbulent voyage down (before soothing into the Gulf Stream), the children all threw up, repeatedly, undeterred by eating green apples, sipping hot consommé and snacking on dry biscuits out of a tin. My mother, at last free of household chores, threw herself on a starboard deck chair, reading Pearl Buck's *The Good Earth*. My father, who had upstaged us by his frequent trips to London to search out his ancestor Thomas Browne (baptized in

Lavenham, Suffolk, in 1605), took refuge in the mahogany bar, sipping Scotch and water and deliberately facing the florid barman so as not to perceive the heaving of the sea. On arrival, we were awake and dressed to view the spectacular operatic entrance into Hamilton harbor, punctuated by the petulant roar of the Monarch, answered, quite bravely, by the piping of the two tugs guiding us into the Furness Front Street Wharf—now jingling, like Babel, with commercial shouts, enthusiastic greetings and unintelligible exclamations. A buzzing Bermudian bazaar.

Now into carriages with kindly drivers in white sun helmets and horses of equal demeanor, we were off with cousin Mignon around the bend at the end of the harbor, alongside the narrow-gauge railroad of lacquered brown and green, clop-clopping faster and faster among the bicycles and horse-drawn carts. In the flash of entry we are inundated with colors never registered before. Blues, greens, pinks, yellows, oranges, white/custard roofs, and pastels from another world. Along the coral roads up the serpentine Crowe Hill by Birdsy's house, alongside Harmony Hall, down by the carriage house (now a beauty parlor), to the left, another swing upward, by St. Paul's Lane, my father imperiously pointing out to us the slender spire of St. Paul's Church where we were to be involuntarily led on Sunday mornings, then by Marshall's grocery (now Modern Mart & Chicken Delight). To the right a moment or two, we come at last to Southcote Cottage (sign at the stone-coral gate) and scurried into the low-slung house to claim our summer quarters. Out in five minutes, in swim suits, running and laughing all the way down to the Elba (public) beach—for our first memorable dunk in the celebrated azure sea.

Bermuda is a diamond necklace, flung on blue-green glass—at one tip is St. George's and St. David's (then a separate island) and at the other, Somerset (out in the country, lawn tennis, white sepulchers, pure white-spired churches and the world's smallest drawbridge, jowled adjacent to the slithering railroad, wending archly to the end).

We saw more of Bermuda in 1937 than we see today, since World War II that is, because the railroad's cheerful conductors allowed us to swing up on our bikes on board and travel the incalculable kilometers to the by-ways and to the ends of the Bermuda earth. We traveled daily this seductive necklace island, incredibly just 500 miles off the North Carolina coast (145 islands, actually, strung with imperceptible bridges, a triple volcano eruption eons ago, struck in a hurricane by the British ship "Sea Venture" and memorialized forever by Shakespeare in *The Tempest*, plunk in the middle of the eerie Sargasso Sea) but, more accurately, perhaps a million beautiful miles from nowhere.

Mark Twain recognized the island as a prelude to Heaven. He failed, however, to see it *as* heaven. You understand, he came down frequently on a schooner (as did my grandmother, Miriam Megargee, on her honeymoon in 1890). Mark Twain stayed at the old clapboard Princess Hotel on Hamilton Harbor, and sometimes in his final three years at the home of the American Vice Consul Allen (whose teenage daughter fascinated him), but always in the winter season—December to March, after which, white-suited, he would retreat to the banalities of Hartford, Connecticut, enjoying his white-headed renown as the Supreme Yankee, Samuel Clemens.

One day riding a steamboat down the Mississippi river to New Orleans he heard the captain shout, "Mark Twain!," indicating, I suppose, the water's depth for the safety of the vessel. He like the authoritative sound of that riverboat expression and adopted it straightaway as his own. But he never felt the passionate spirit inculcated on youthful souls by a visit to Bermuda in the blessed summertime. His loss.

My brother George and I that sweet summer fifty years ago used to imagine we were pirates. With spears in hand, noses and shoulders raw with sunburn, glass masks and flippers in tow, we would swim out off Elba beach to an amber-rusted wrecked ship, inside the reef. There in the spooky stillness of light and shadow, waving coral plants about us, we discovered, not treasures of gold and silver, but rather two remarkable moray eels—each five glistening feet long—one green and one black. Slithering in a corner of the captain's cabin, now deep under water, we were fascinated by their cat-like grins, exhibiting to our pleasure and our horror innumerable sharp needle teeth. It was macho in those salad days to foolishly poke the vicious morays until our bursting lungs compelled return to the surface for gasps of air after which we would return for more mischief. Before the summer was over, my brother had lost his best front tooth in a struggle with me underwater at the wreck, now gone forever.

These magical reefs, the magnificent other world under sea, sparkling with the polish of the radiant sun, provided daily eight-hour voyages of wonder for us. We made friends with Disney-like fish (605 species in these waters including grouper, chub, wahoo, marlin, tuna, dolphin, bonefish and amberjack, as well as the frightened flickering silversides). The parrot fish were more predictable than the moray, less tricky and explosive than Bobby the Baracuda, who whisked around off Coral Beach midway to the ominous big reef where more than rumor told of man-biting sharks, lurking sullenly for a feast of young sun-cooked flesh. Considering the time George and I spent underwater, sometimes led by Malcolm Martin and John Hornburg, it is not surprising that we came upon a shark or two and with utter naive adventurism would pursue them, haughtily, in the fashion of the Light Brigade, armed with our clumsy rusted spears. We never once speared a shark or caught a barracuda. I shudder at my movie-set recollections. At the time we pretended to be brave.

Returning to Bermuda many times over the years, the mind's eye records the changes and the changeless as well. Sale of the grand and gracious railroad to Paraguay for a cargo of Argentine beef and a case of Johnny Walker Black Label; paving of the inimitable coral back roads in the name of progress; arrival of ubiquitous small automobiles like ants across a barn door, affecting inevitably the culture, pace and romance of an Impressionistic idyl so loved by Winslow Homer. Gone were the Monarch and the Queen, sacrificed to World War II as troop carriers; gone were the little hot grocery stores along the south shore roads: canned goods, green-bottled beer with a neat label in sharp black and red, "Brauerei Beck & Co.-Bremen, Germany—*Beck's Bier*," but no ice for Cokes or beer, yet always an enormous English wheel of cheese, like a millstone, covered with an opaque glass cover and knob. The rich flavor of the steaming cheese escaped from around the cover and fetidly flavored the store with an earthiness remembered a half-century later as if yesterday.

My vivacious sisters, Harriett and Bebe, were sufficiently thrilled with the romance of the dulcet Bermuda breezes, soft colors, lapis lazuli sea, and sweet flowering trees that they became receptive to the ardent pursuits of various American and Bermudian swains. One was an English-trained architect still active on the island today. Another was a blonde graduate of Yale who my father slyly introduced as the Captain of the Yale varsity crew "defeated at Henley." He responded to this dig with the droll insouciance "aha . . . " of James Stewart in the movie "Philadelphia Story."

In those days romance was triggered in the glorious outdoor hotel dancing pavilions with huge concrete leafs within which a twelve-piece orchestra played waltzes, fox trots and sambas to the delight of light-footed elbow-jerking young couples, she with deep dips and dresses like lampshades; he with Vasolined hair, white pants, and if very preppy, red yacht slacks.

Demanding to know precisely where his daughters were spending the evening with their boyfriends, my father would at Southcote suggest to me that we pay an investigatory visit to the dancing open-air palaces at Elbow Beach Hotel, Inverurie or Belmont. Riding on bicycles like commandos over the cool coral roads, my father in white hunter's helmet and bermuda shorts, we would sneak up on the band-ignited revelers and try to identify my sisters, whom they were with, what they were doing and, more especially, whether they had limited themselves to Coca-Cola or, at the outside, claret and lemonade. We rarely, if ever, discovered perfidy and would return silently the way we had come to Southcote. And so to bed.

Endless energetically-planned family trips to Devil's Hole, the Perfume Factory, the Crystal Caves, underwater thrills in Harrington Sound, the Aquarium to photograph sand sharks and moray eels, St. David's lighthouse, over to and up the steps of cast-iron Gibbs light

overlooking "Waterlot" where my father took me to meet
raconteur restaurateur Claudia Darrell with her red hair
flying, who told us a hundred tales of the island (some of
them true); to Hamilton to shop—Trimingham's,
H.A.&E. Smith, A. S. Cooper, the book store, century-
old Bluck's, Gosling Brothers, over to the esteemed
Twenty-One Bar, overlooking the cruise ships—very smart
to be there, my oldest sister insisted. "Everyone is *here,*"
she said, sipping a dark rum and Coca-Cola. To the right,
ferries cobwebbing the places to go and to visit. Discussions
as to whether the place was worth seeing but, as Samuel
Johnson discerned, was it worth *going* to see? Bike trips to
St. George's (my father loved history and here it was).
"Look, Peter, this church [reading] was established in 1727.
Can you imagine that?" I said, "No, I can't."

Back in late afternoon we pushed our bikes uphill
under firecracker bowers of poinciana trees, the birds
shrieking and the roads dusty with beige in the denoue-
ment of the long day. The climate is cozy and warm.
Evening is sensed in the rise of the breeze, but not before
my father has an enterprising idea for all of us. "Why don't
we skirt into Hamilton for a cool moment in the Quarry
Bar?" No one dissented. We knew there, high on Hamilton
hills, was a special place—200 feet down from street level,
300 steps below, cut in coral stone, was a quarried-out bar,
cool as a cucumber, hospitable cedar wood bar, and there,
bless the owner, was cold German beer, cold Coca-Cola,
cold lemonade and a moment of peace to contemplate the
day. Until my mother, long disenchanted with the gloomy
ambiance of the Quarry Bar, would say, "Well, let's go
home to Southcote."

We then took our bikes on the ferry from the foot
of where the policemen in helmets at midday directed
traffic of carriages and carts and dignified bicyclers. The

carriage horses wore straw hats. Everyone wore hats in those days of 1937 when the Japanese sank the U.S.S. Panay and isolationism was at its peak.

The day had ended, yes, but not its joyous counterpart—the jeweled nighttime in Bermuda, as beautiful and as exciting as day. At Elbow Beach, Eddie Wittstein and his "Yale Prom Orchestra" played "I Dreamt That I Dwelt in Marble Halls." The sounds drifted up, feathered by the soft-rising and falling of the wind. Crickets creaked in rising crescendo.

After experimentation as meticulous as a research physician, my father finally settled on Gosling "Black Seal" rum as his favorite evening toddy on the Southcote terrace, overlooking a garden gone to seed. His digestive system had been insensibly destroyed on the New York Stock Exchange where he had a seat but never sat. October 1929 and subsequent dreary down-grading depression years took their livid toll of his vascular system and his tender colon. So he was naturally delighted to discover that Gosling rum brought incomparable euphoria to an anxious and beleagured spirit. He hit upon a plan to import a case or two to New York and in this way to carry the grace and well-being directly to his home environment in New York City. The Bermuda rum was duly delivered. For the next week or so he sampled and tippled his treasure, but, alas, once back in the dreadful stock market on Wall Street, among the bears, his old suffering returned despite the medicinal black bottles of Gosling in his library closet.

Half of life is memory. It is not a chronological video, good and bad flickering on screen. It is, I think, edited patches and flashes, recollections sudden and precise as the prick of a pin. We dream much of it. How satisfying, how truly marvelous to have, by sheer luck, that special summer in Bermuda, at another distant time.

What is particularly exquisite to the visitor from Carnegie Hill, where I continue to live in New York, is the sanctuary Bermuda still is. Sheltered so pridefully by an Olympian-minded government and the warm-hearted people. Where we came in 1937 (where I am as I write this retrospection) is the Paget Parish area of Elba and Coral beach on the incomparable south shore. It was perfect. It is the same—to which all six senses attest. (The sixth is appreciation). Our family, new generations, are back again to savor, to remember and enjoy. We read, we write, we love.

There is still the tooth rock at the end of Coral Beach, our birds-eye cat-bird table up on a terrace, the curved, turreted lookout at 180 degrees of rare seascape bathed in light and painted atmosphere blue. Palms sway over us with dignity, dressed in stripped skins of rough brown-greys, against the profile of red-veined bay grape leaves, undulating lazily over Persian azure seas. Out beyond is the honest cold cobalt waters where hazy tankers roam. Just as at the beginning the waves, protected by the reefs, slip in to the shoreline to curtsy nicely and retreat. These gentle waves of white embroidery do not crash or thunder as in Maine or Portugal. They glide as in a ballet, with grace, murmuring to us of peace and holiday.

The clouds are still English clouds—up high, moving or stationary, (Arabic writings) across the horizon, often sprinkled with cinnamon, and escorted by puffy pilots in grey. These of course were painted there long ago by Constable at another serene time. Contrasted in texture into deep third dimensions, somehow transposed by the Greek light and the heavenly repose.

The pink sands are still for children, and grandchildren, inconducive to the heat of the strong summer sun. Bermudians love their natural blessings. Their silken voice tones reflect their gratitude for this special spirit of place.

We know the silent sanctuary of the day. As Plato mused,

"Based on the crystalline sea
Of thought and its eternity."

A half century of beauty and real liveliness begun one special summer in Bermuda long ago.

–III–

REFLECTIONS ON THE BIG CRASH

Following are excerpts from an open letter written October 23, 1987, to my father, George Estabrook Brown, a stockbroker, who died in 1946—exhausted by the market's exasperating low behavior following seventeen dreadful years since the Big Crash of October, 1929:

On Monday, October 19, 1987, now labelled Black Monday, I appeared on ABC Radio's "The Bob Grant Show"—live—for an hour's interview, presumably about my new book, *The Art of Questioning*. At about 3:20 p.m., a studio agent invaded the broadcasting room interrupting Bob Grant with a written note and an expression of catastrophe. The note said, in effect, "The Stock Market has fallen out of bed—DOWN 500 points. No buyers. *Free fall!*" Hand shaking, the agent shouted this message even though Grant's show was "on the air."

Excited by the revelation and oblivious of his guest, Bob Grant, shifting gears, started to convey this awful news to the listening public throughout the metropolitan area.

Looking through the microphone at my host, I felt the surge of electric intensity that comes to us in moments of impending disaster affecting the lives of everyone around, in all walks of life. No one had any idea of what was happening or what to expect. The puzzlement was enormous—unreal—and my mouth went dry.

Suddenly, silence in the studio. Bob Grant looked through his microphone across the table at his guest. The messenger had departed as quickly as he had come in.

"Well, now, Mr. Brown, I invited you here to discuss your book about asking the right questions, and now I'm going on with the audience about the sudden plunge of the stock market. I'm sure you don't want to talk about that!"

"Oh, yes, I do, Bob," I replied. "I'd be glad to talk about the stock market crash. That's about all I ever talked about with my father from October, 1929 on.

"Are you serious?" Grant said.

"Yes. My father had a seat on the New York Stock Exchange—although he never sat down. He came to Wall Street in the boom of the mid-twenties, witnessed first-hand the Crash of 1929, the panic and the aftermath that lasted for a horrible decade and more."

•   •   •

This is roughly what happened on Black Monday to introduce me to a plunge of the Dow Jones average of almost 25% of its value—worse than the worst day of October, 1929. This took me back to our conversations in the early days of the Great Depression, hard on the heels of the Great Crash. So, pen in hand, I write this letter to you. You came home to our apartment high on Carnegie

Hill early as there was a dearth of actual business to do, and I came home early from a young grade at school where there was no afternoon study.

You said that Herbert Hoover had insisted that the fundamental condition of the American economy in the Fall of 1929 was strong. All good people said the same. All would be well. Hang in there. John D. Rockefeller said the next day, after Black Thursday, October 29, 1929, that fundamental conditions of the country are strong and that there is nothing in the business situation to warrant destruction of values that had taken place. In fact, Mr. Rockefeller announced that he and his son for some days had been purchasing sound common stocks. You recalled to me that the radio comedian Eddie Cantor, having heard this, declared: "Well, why not. They are the only ones with any money."

President Hoover, with hair parted in the middle and looking like an Arrow shirt ad, was reluctant to alarm a panicky American public. You said he had chosen not to call the unhappy economic condition in 1930–31 a "recession" as this was too *harsh* an indictment of the situation. Better to call it a milder easier-to-recover name such as a mere "depression." The word stuck and as the economic disaster deepened and spread to the horrors of lost funds, lost savings, lost homes and farms to foreclosures and drought, the American public began to call the situation "The Great Depression" which lingers ominously into these times.

One difference this week is the way some financial big shots boast openly they got out of the stock market before Monday's plunge—even so far as making a killing buying up stocks now at bargain-basement prices. "I got out at the top" is a cry never heard in 1929. Later, rumor had it that some had avoided the Niagara-like plunge over the falls, such as Joseph P. Kennedy and Bernard Baruch. But for the most part, the big investors took a virtual patriotic stance that their own buying efforts must shore up the rushing descent of stock prices. You always reminded me that George F. Baker, grand financier (whose steely-eyed portrait is still on the staircase of the Harvard Club) had in 1931 gotten out of a sick bed to go down to the Exchange to buy. His valiant efforts failed and unhappily the stock market plunged again, to depths that persuaded you that 1931 was the cruelist blow of all.

This week modern titans (called entrepreneurs) told of their success in evading the market's treacherous decline—the likes of Donald J. Trump, real estate tycoon and would-be statesman from Queens; T. Boone Pickens, Jr., who likes mergers and acquisitions, and that master of the takeover of American companies, Carl C. Icahn.

Another difference is the attitude of Wall Street toward government intervention. You told me few of the financial leaders, if any, desired or called for aid from Washington. What could be done was available from private resources and private initiative. J. P. Morgan, star of plugging financial dikes, had died in 1913. In 1929 his son, inheritor of his mantle, was in Europe. At the Morgan company, a Morgan partner called a meeting of the private sector financial leadership. The President of the New York Stock Exchange, Richard Whitney, led the delegation optimistically to the U.S. Steel trading post where he dramatically bought shares above the market. The brave effort failed and the downward wash continued.

You had a small office in the apartment off the kitchen with a roll top walnut desk inherited from your father. Over the desk was a framed gold-embossed certificate of your admission as a member to the New York Stock Exchange. I remember the certificate recounted high standards of dealings necessary on the illustrious Exchange and the character and "integrity" required for sustaining membership. The certificate bore the flourished signature of the President—"Richard Whitney"—who, a few months later, in 1935, went to Sing Sing prison for embezzlement and fraud.

The head of Sears, Roebuck as the 1929 debacle hit Wall Street, in a typical mind-set of the times, offered to "guarantee" the stock market accounts of his almost 50,000 employees. A surprisingly large part of the public were "in the market" which had been exploding upward since the mid-twenties. Part of the lure was the slim requirement of only 10% down for margin. Ordinary folks had begged, borrowed and mortgaged to buy these fast-rising stocks on margin as if there would be no end to prosperity. Illusions fed on themselves.

You had a favorite book you told me about during the Depression: *Popular Delusions and the Madness of Crowds*. There was a short foreword written in succinct and knowing style by the wizard of Wall Street, Bernard Baruch. Here was a man who understood the psychology of the stock markets: when a trader *desperately* wanted to sell his asset to Mr. Baruch, he would buy; when someone *desperately* wanted to buy an asset owned by Mr. Baruch, he would sell. Either way this canny, agreeable man made enormous profits. The book itself, I remember, had fascinating stories of presumed historic fact about the Dutch Tulip Mania—when Persian bulbs rose in value to thousands of dollars in guilders. On one occasion a cook in a rich merchant's household mistook a rare and valuable tulip bulb for an ordinary onion and threw it in the evening stew. Another story traced the rise and fall in England of investors entrapped by enthusiasm and greed in the South Sea Bubble. Another—the Crusaders of the Middle Ages (including the Children's Crusade—that never returned from the ill-fated journey) and the esoterics of European rage for the St. Vitus Dance. We marvelled, smugly, about the foolish impulses of mankind. We felt sure that never again would we be a part of such popular delusions and madness of crowds.

What you reminded me of was the irritating fact that everyone, in such times, whether in the stock market or not, is a loser, one way or another. You told of company officers and brokers literally selling apples. I recall the unemployed executive, reduced from haughtiness, standing in back of a fruit box on which were placed apples, well polished, and a sign which said: *"Apples, 5¢."* The bread lines and the soup kitchens were daily realities in the thirties. The mood was grey-brown. People wore grey-brown suits, often second-hand, and in our family, passed down. I never quite got to the point where I appreciated my older brother's taste in grey and brown. My mother explained that this color would not show the dirt.

The stock market had become, after October, 1929, a bell-wether of all unhappy public response. The downfall of the securities market affected in turn the price of other things, personal as well as real property. Those assets that necessitated maintenance of any kind plummeted in value to a point—you had startling examples among friends—where the black Buick, the Chris Craft speedboat, the hunting lodge, the house at Cap d'Antibe, the Elco family yacht docked in Bay Shore, the courtly Greenwich estate, the duplex on Fifth Avenue, were *given* away. Here, take it off my hands, please!

It did not seem strange at the time to you or to me that in the '20s and early '30s no one had (1) Social Security, (2) medical assistance, (3) bank insurance on deposits to $100,000, (4) regulatory agencies watch-dogging financial markets, (5) farmers and farms protection from foreclosure and drought, (6) banking stability—on the contrary, the banks were surrounded by panicked depositors. The run on banks' funds caused them to drop like flies and the first thing that happened when F.D.R. became President in March 1933 (41 months *after* the Big Crash), was to close down the banks.

The President then began planning the economic recovery for America in such depth and pervasive reach as to astound you and your generation. To your chagrin the younger generation saw the government regulation revolution of the New Deal as experimentally exciting and necessary. The country was obviously hurting and that's about all people talked about. I remember you were not at all pleased to see me leave for Browning School one October morning in 1932 sporting a large red, white and blue button imprinted in black letters, "VOTE FOR F.D.R." Your disgust, I must say, did not rise to the level you exhibited when in 1938 you caught me in the library reading "The Daily Worker."

The detailed frustration, panic and anxious loss in the pit of the stomach was not experienced by me in 1929 when I was seven, but rather vicariously felt later on in conversations with you and others. This time around—October 1987—the impact is direct to the solar plexis. Whether you have a bundle invested or not, you still feel the frightening final hour of freefall on Monday.

The financial page of *The New York Times* on October 20, 1987 showed a graph of the market activity

27

the previous day. It was a line—*straight down*, as long as a pencil. A free fall like a rock. All the sages tell us, rather emphatically, the world will never be the same again. Of course you told me exactly the same thing in the thirties. Possibly both can be true.

One thing seems unfair this time. For the media to place all its fierce blame on the President—as it did, as the public did, last time. To blame the President alone for the willful illusions of millions of Americans and eager foreign investors seems somewhat absurd. After all, the United States government greatly reduced inflation and unemployment. At the same time we have the horrendous hangover of public debt (you will not believe) from an extensive period of spend, spend, spend (elect, elect, elect!) and a terribly high international trade deficit making our prideful country a debtor nation! You told me the stock market shift, up or down, is always explained in retrospect. "Oh, there is profit-taking." "Oh, interest rates may be rising." "Oh, the Dictator of the Soviets won't come over to talk to us." Had the market not precipitously broken, there would be no cause to trot out these excuses. You said as a rule all was a matter of personal *confidence* in the day-to-day future. If confidence dissolves, the downward sell-off are set in place.

The other day a Wall Street investor, known for his acumen, was asked: "Why has the stock market gone down so abruptly?" He responded: "Well, I'll tell you. It may sound like a cliché, but when the market goes *down*, it goes *down*." You related once that during a panic or two earlier in our history, J. P. Morgan was asked as he left his office at 23 Wall Street: "Excuse me, Mr. Morgan, please tell us what the stock market is going to do?" J. P. Morgan

28

stopped a moment, looked over his bulbous nose with staring eyes and replied: "What it *always* does. Goes up and goes down . . . "

Excessive is a fair characteristic of the 1929 crash and excessive is a fair characteristic of the 1987 crash. As *Time* Magazine trumpeted, in the same manner it recorded the last Big Crash in 1929, "Now it's the morning after, and the dream of painless prosperity has been punctured. But what a wild binge it was! Speculative fortunes built on junk bonds and stock manipulations helped paper over the cracks in an economy beset by sluggish investment and productivity. Some of the best minds of a generation marched off to make millions as market mavens, embracing the greed-and-glory smugness that suffused Wall Street and Washington. An economy that was once based on manufacturing might and inventive genius began pursuing wealth through mergers and takeovers and the creation of new financial instruments. Fortunes were conjured out of thin air by fresh-faced traders who created nothing more than paper-gilded castles in the sky held aloft by red suspenders."

The young, arrogant moneymanagers (who never experienced the Big Depression) were severely castigated. These crestfallen dealers are labeled "Yuppies" and the story makes the rounds that the difference between them and a pigeon is that they now can't make a deposit on a BMW.

Well, the second Crash on Monday startled me, and recalled so vividly and so poignantly the melancholies of the last time around that devoured your own time and energy and wonder. You shared with me so often your own feelings and your concerns about what to do "next time" that I thought I'd write to remember those days long ago arising from the ashes of the last Great Crash, and report, I guess, that we didn't learn very much.

Affectionately,
PETER

–IV–

FAMILY ODYSSEY TO GREECE

Standing out in my memory today—run and rerun over again in my recollection—is a brief visit our family made to the Greek Mediterranean fourteen years ago.

Alexandra and I wanted to take with us the three children still at home—Nathaniel (13), Alexandra II (8) and Brooke (5). We wanted to explore the Mediterranean basin of our civilization and spiritual roots. We wanted to experience, to feel, Greece's peninsula, its Aegean islands as well as Alexandria and Cairo, ending up, quietly, on the island of Corfu on the Ionian sea, off the boot of Italy, for a final rest and reflection before returning to the stress and cacophony of New York.

Alexandra and I shared a notion that a visit with family to this time-capsule cradle of world history would provide insights for all of us about life's meaning, how to sustain our spirit over the years and how perhaps to contemplate the purpose of life on earth and beyond.

We couldn't afford the trip but everyone consulted was positive about the adventure and the children agreed to contribute what savings they had stored up. We were partners.

So many friends and elders hearing of our planned odyssey to Greece were appalled that we chose to take with us "the children." They were "too young," they would remember nothing," it was "sinfully wasteful"—why not go alone? How wrong they were. We all found our journey together to Greece a high point of our lives—learning about life—so quick and over—and learning about ourselves.

"Other countries may offer you discoveries in manners or love or landscape," said novelist Lawrence Durrell, "Greece offers you something harder—*the discovery of yourself.*"

We gathered our three children around us one evening in New York and set down the terms of our travel to Greece. First, everyone would keep a *diary* (tangible memory!)—every day—no falling behind! Second, everyone would be helpful, cheerful, travel lightly (one suitcase each) and no getting sick. By the grace of the Lord, this plan worked out and everyone had notebooks of the holiday in the Mediterranean, legible enough to discern the reaction of each of the five (53 years to five) to the sights and scenes we all experienced.

There should be no generational problem in this overseas project for wisdom is a broad spectrum. Yesterday I came across these diaries, tucked away in a low drawer in the library, about this exploration over a decade ago (when we were all considerably younger). My mind exploded with the memories of those few days, so vivid and colorful as if yesterday, so abrupt in instruction that these experiences together had literally made us all grow, emotionally, intellectually and as human beings. We had in some way touched, in this beautiful and antique area of the world, a few truths that made life more enjoyable, more precious, perhaps more meaningful. The children's varied reactions gave dimension, sometimes even poignancy.

From this experience, I would recommend that should we do it again in another place, that we would (1) take the children (or grandchildren?)—they are sponges and also *teach* us a lot. (2) have them *write it down*— their observations, their thoughts. Forget that we all are not Harvard scholars. Just write it down, as we see it, as one goes along. Reading today what Brooke at age five felt about first seeing the Parthenon gave me a bolt of insight and enthusiasm I've not had for years. Our family regimen was to read avidly about where we'd go next and discuss it, around the table, without talking down, so everyone in the family advanced together, participating equally in the thrill of expectation and fulfillment.

We were seeking somehow literature of the spirit. The joy in this process cannot be easily duplicated by Coney Island rollercoasters, rock band concerts, or flash video of Rambo IV. The bonus I find is that years later (years and years later even more so) you have within you the indescribable gift of the memory of those sweet days. Those days of love and learning, that no one—no autocrat, torturer or terrorist—can take away from you. The memories you have absorbed are the richness of your life.

What we found I think as we look back was not so much discovery of the meaning of life as what Joseph Campbell termed the "experience of being alive." As he would say, we heard a little of the song of the universe and the music of the spheres—"music we dance to even when we cannot name the tune."

The family on this voyage to the Mediterranean recorded their own experiences in their diaries which I hold in my hand. Diaries serve to frame our memory. An advertisement in the *New York Times* one day seduced our family to make this trip together in the summer of 1975. We were told, in luring copy, that Greece was 1,417 golden islands basking in the warm sun where we could marvel at the "towering Parthenon bathed in the silvery Athenian moonlight" and hear the "echoes of 4,000 years of history."

Brooke, age 5, made her first diary entry as follows: "Mommy had shown me pictures of Greece before we came. I was most excited about going on the big boat. I thought Greece would have white stone houses, blue blue blue blue blue sky and blue blue blue blue *blue* water. The sun will be big and bursting and yellow and shining."

Greece and the Mediterranean became for us a unique and exciting experience in our three-week, non-package dash through history. What happened had a curious and perhaps permanent impact on our lives.

I tried to figure out the reason for the magnetism of the Mediterranean for a New York family living 5,000 miles away. Many things that happened to us are indescribable. Travel in this area is a journey through time. For even the youngest, history—so dry and uncompromising—becomes alive and exciting. We climb the Acropolis, touch the Parthenon, swim in a translucent blue bay in sight of the magnificent Temple to Poseidon at Sunion, taste honest vine-ripened tomatoes, savor skewered lamb and veal washed down with lemonade or a fresh Demestica Greek wine, enter the Queen's private apartment in the Palace of Knossos in Northern Crete, pat the five-foot thick fortifications of the Knights of St. John at Rhodes, see with new eyes the dawn come up at sea and the sunset from the looming islands, sit at outside tables in small towns and villages while life throbs around us and look bedazzled at the cliffs of Santorini, the dignified coastlines and the incomparable wine-dark sea. You feel Greece. It is a sensual place.

Greece is a child's paradise. No station wagon, no peanut butter, no routine, no separate schedules, no obnoxious "sacrifices" for the children. A summer Mediterranean journey in a few days implants more real education than years of summer school in the States. Here in Greece are the bones on which the flesh can grow. The pure air, indigo sea, food from the earth, breathless scenery as the head turns, all combine somehow to make the inculcation of this education joyful to both body and spirit. We returned renewed, with a fresh eye to life.

Tourmaster Thomas Cook a hundred years ago urged a family holiday as an *intellectual* experience, an instrument "for the advancement of mankind"—something other, I suppose, than all-night topless discotheque frolics at packaged paradises off Morocco, Tahiti or the Costa del Sol. Cook may have had an idea whose time has come. Why not a family holiday together in an environment where even the dullest or youngest cannot help but return more enlightened, more aware of one's identity and goals? Should such decision be made, there is no better summer place to do it, I think, than in the Greek Mediterranean—even today with the current risks of pop-up terrorists, striking randomly here and there.

•   •   •

After arrival in Athens, Alexandra I (mother), entered in her diary for August 10, a Saturday, blessed with a sunny blue sky:

"When we arrived and entered the quarry of the breathtaking Parthenon through the Propylaia, Brooke wanted to know why everything was all broken. We told her about the wars and bombs. She said it was terrible other countries would bomb the Greek's good things and buildings. One of the first experiences we had was a Dutch woman telling me my wraparound skirt was blowing in the breeze and you can see everything. For her sake, we found a safety pin.

"When something is most meaningful to you it intensifies the experience to see it through someone else's eyes—especially the eyes of those you love. Knowing Peter, Nathaniel, Alexandra II (daughter), and Brooke had never seen the Parthenon made me feel twice as moved—tenfold!

"This time for me, my third trip to Greece, was no disappointment. We sat on a bench looking at this building and Peter asked me if it changed any, and I said 'no, but I have.' I saw new beauty in proportion and line I hadn't fully appreciated before. The Parthenon is the most graceful subtle building I've ever seen. Walking around the building, seeing it from all angles makes you feel the marble breathing. We could see *through* the buildings from our hotel and when we saw the hill and the buildings lit up at night, it looks like a jewel through the darkness. The experience hit us all. Peter said he *is* Greek—Truth and Beauty; Beauty and Truth."

For the *same* visit Brooke's (age 5) entry in her diary was:

"I like the Parthenon the best. The whole mountain, the whole thing. The bombing was terrible. It's not nice to do that to somebody else's building. It's not nice to do bad things to other people. It still looks pretty, bombed, but it isn't nice to do."

The following day we travelled to Cape Sunion at the southernmost tip of the Greek peninsula in Attica to visit longtime Greek friends. Nathaniel (age 13) recorded:

"So we left Athens on our trip in a taxi that was driven by an English-speaking Greek who gave us a tour as we traveled along the 'new' shore road. We passed many hotels and beaches. As we left, our driver Gus told me I was a classic and looked like a Greek god—very interesting. The driver was an accredited tour guide and associated Greek and Roman myths. I couldn't believe it—we passed the Lyceum where Socrates taught Plato."

Continued Nathaniel's (age 13) diary:

"Arrived in Sunion, in the south tip of Attica below Athens, and the intense blue of the sky and the white house of our Greek friends against deep blue of the sea was magnifique. We greeted our host and his family and had a lunch of fresh grilled fish and salad, all very Greek. Then after lunch we went down to the water to a small cove. No sand beach but a natural place to get into the water. I love to swim and I brought my snorkeling equipment along and was the first in the water.

"The water was so beautiful. It was the first time I had ever been in the Aegean Sea. I swam around many rocks and small caves and found one cave with an opening at both ends and went through several times from both directions. Then I went in and stopped to look around inside a bit and noticed a kind of fauna on the rocks in one place which was an intense orange and purple. I was amazed at the beauty of it!

"As we walked back to the house we saw Gus, the driver, was waiting. We dressed and left with another friend of our host and were off—with Sunion only as memory. We traveled back on what Gus called the 'old' road through the 'inside' country. Very beautiful getting another aspect of the outskirts of Athens."

The next excerpt recorded here is when we went to board the Stella *Oceanis*, the Sun Line ship that would take us across the Aegean Sea, together, for seven days.

The diary of Alexandra II (age 8) reflects:

Tuesday, August 12:

"At sea in the Aegean all day enroute to Alexandria, Egypt . . . This was a great day. We perked up immediately when we saw the pool filled and discovered there were some children our age who spoke English. At breakfast we saw a family with a girl about my and Brooke's age. Later by the pool Brooke asked me if I'd introduce her—Lori, now living in West Africa, originally from Seattle, Washington, age 7. Quickly, I was in the act and from that moment on we girls were like Flopsy, Mopsy and Cottontail. We never knew for sure where we were but we knew we were together. We played Prince and Princess, swam, and went down to our cabin and giggled."

My diary entry speaks of extraordinary Greek light—sharp and pure:

"Contrasts with the diaphonous softness of the light of Spain and France. In Greece atmosphere is clean and strong. The extra dimension of the Greek Mediterranean is the light. *Xenos* (stranger or guest) only learns upon arrival what depth and meaning the ineffable light has upon the land and seascape. Dazzling, sparkly as spring water, dawn-of-creation clearness, showing absolute relief. Artificiality cannot exist in this mysterious light. From Rhodes to Corfu, daylight or moonlight, Greek light bathes this world in a special timeless beauty, enough to wring some ounce of philosophy and love from the most stubborn itinerant, young and old.

"Nikos Kazankzakis recognized the factor of Greek light in his classic *Zorba, the Greek:*

'The sea . . . islands bathed in light . . . happy is the man . . . who, before dying, has the good fortune to sail the Aegean Sea.'

"The light in the sky varies imperceptibly and quickly—cool-bright, gentle pinks and violets, tints of blue, patches of brilliant white and gold, and then folds of aubergine, intense and leadening as night nears. Dawn is trumpets heralding rebirth. Sunsets in Greece are glorious fourths of July, for in summer there is unbroken sunshine."

Diary entry at sea: "Henry Miller in Crete saw the blue sky shading up into the ultimate light which makes everything Greek seem holy, nocturnal and familiar. 'In Greece,' he said once, 'one has the desire to bathe in the sky.' "

•　　　•　　　•

Finally after a trip through Egypt's port city, Alexandria, we arrived four hours later on a bus in 104-degree heat at Cairo's Egyptian Museum. We were hot and we were tired. The five of us were long in love with the sea and if we had a choice would prefer to be at the water's edge. The children were disenchanted to come in to a dark and dusty museum, almost dreary to look at—sticks and stones and broken old bones and mummies. Brooke pleaded, "Do we have to?" It was crowded and the visiting group was large, yet each of us responded to the unique treasures inside: Tutenkamen's exquisite treasures, elaborate death masks and objects found inside his tomb, so refined and detailed that Alexandra said she felt that modern designers had repeatedly borrowed all that is true and beautiful—purity of line and form—from early Egyptian discoveries. This was true of so many objects we observed—a comb, a slingback chair, the jewelry, the blind hinges—imagine, over 3,000 years ago! (Later I learned that the corn found in the tomb still can be popped today . . .)

Within a year or so these precious objects, with much fanfare, were transported to the Metropolitan Museum of Art on Fifth Avenue in New York City for a bombastic show, clean and well-lit. The lines outside to get in were endless for months. It interested me that the children, their appetites whetted, were as excited about the New York presentation of the same treasures.

When we arrived aboard our ship at the Greek island of Rhodes, Alexandra's one entry was:

"In the Greek world Rhodes is as far southeast from Corfu as you can get. These waters are clear greens merging into blues, foam lit with phosphorescence from within.

"We walked through time. The 15th Century old city with pebbled streets of the Knights of St. John stirred our imagination of long long ago.

"In the Rhodes' archaeological museum all of us were excited by the Romanesque setting and the wealth of sculpture and vases. The museum was once the Hospital of the Knights."

Daughter Alexandra II's diary: "The two statues that thrilled me were the *Marine Venus* and *Aphrodite*. The Marine Venus was found underwater; she is warm, soft, full of grace. Brookie and Mother love to touch in order to feel. We were glad to be able to walk around these pieces and see and examine them so closely—to feel their marble bodies inhaling.

"Aphrodite is graceful and smooth: In Brooke's words, 'comfortable.' Art history has always been of special interest to mother since it was introduced so warmly in 1956 by her wonderful teacher at Mary A. Burnham School, Phyl Gardner. This subject is of endless fascination, she says, because in all periods of history throughout civilization there has been a code which goes beyond to embellish and ornament for beauty and pleasure. Mother says an example of this is the early stone man whose tools were ornamented with such detail that one needs a microscope to see the subtle designs."

Nathaniel (age 13) continued:

"Last year I was in the 7th Grade at St. Bernard's where I took Greek History. I studied with a great teacher the Myth of Theseus and the reality of the myth for over a month.

"I was so glad to be going to Knossos because then I would really be able to see that fantastic civilization.

"We gulped down some sort of breakfast and boarded our English-speaking bus with our guide, Lolita. The drive to Knossos was only some fifteen minutes and we were there where the modern civilization lived in 1600 B.C. when all of Europe except for Crete, I'm told, was still in the barbaric state.

"We saw the throne room of the palace, the amazing plumbing system, the king's and queen's bedrooms and toilets, with baths supplied with hot water. It was *unbelievable*. Also the frescoes were magnificent: pictures of fish and dolphins with such beauty as cannot be imagined.

"The system of lighting was fantastic. A light well that illuminated all the apartments in the palace—so complicated it was called the 'labyrinth' in the Myth of Theseus.

"There was a small shop where we could buy post-cards and pamphlets about the historic sites. As we left we passed the pits in which the plates and pottery which were considered sacred were put when broken. The memory of Knossos will remain as vivid as it did one minute after we left under the grape arbor."

On the same scene, my diary reflects:

"Of the temples that still survive, many have the first blush appearance of a construction site—messy, roof-less and robbed; pilfered ages past of their furniture and treasure, prostrate and numb, destined to be tread by end-less tourists wending their mindless ways. Official guards on the whole are apparently selected for having not the slightest interest in their quarry. Americans in particular seem over-excited by the plumbing as if this leap in engi-neering by the Minoans somehow establishes the high ide-als of our own civilization across 3,600 years.

"Most exciting see of Crete is the Palace of Minos at Knossos (pronounced No-sauce!); its discovery was a wonder event of the 20th Century. Sir Arthur Evans, an English gentleman, gave himself and his fortune to a con-troversial restoration—reconstruction of fallen parts, res-toration of frescoes and sculptures. By careful reconstruc-tion he gave to the visitor today a more vivid picture of how royalty lived in the heyday of ancient Crete. This civili-zation continued for a thousand years.

"The Palace lies a few moments south of the mid-north City of Heraklion where we docked on schedule at 10 a.m. The Palace stands atop a small hill, Kefaia, above the banks of a river dry in summer but large enough for transportation to the town. The view from the Palace is comparable to the center valley of Corfu—cypresses, green and straight up, olive trees galore (it was an olive grove Sir Arthur had to buy out) and graceful rolling vineyards.

"Difficult to believe that surrounding this Palace was the capital city of Crete harboring a population of over 100,000. Homer sang of 90 cities of Crete. Today archeologists have uncovered more than 100, which of course proves that Homer was incapable of exaggeration. None of these cities had a wall. Sea power was sufficient. Crete maintained the peace for a millennium in the Aegean, from which flowered unprecedented prosperity and art.

"A major reason Crete prospered so during the Minoan period over other Aegean Islands and cities was its active trade with Egypt. Going to Alexandria and to Cairo helped us fit together some of the puzzling pieces of the Mediterranean past.

"About 1700 B.C. the Palace was destroyed by a stunning blow, most likely an earthquake caused by eruption of the Santorini (Thera) Volcano named Thiria. Out of the horrendous destruction a new indomitable civilization grew up, more beautiful and stronger than ever, a harbinger of the Hellenic classical civilization, and in turn we hope our own.

"To an ordinary family of five living in an apartment in Manhattan, what makes an on-foot inspection of the Minoan Palace so exciting: the restoration lets you step into the apartments themselves—windows and balconies overlooking a magnificent view; ingenious passages and staircases; carefully planned shafts of light as well as openings to regular breezes for constant air-conditioning; a drainage system envied by architects today; drinking water conduits and those for washing as well showed fastidiousness unrecognized in many places we now go. The drinking water came from a hill above, ultimately by aquaducts; the apartments we saw were decorated in such vivid colors as Pompeiian red. We were surprised to find relentless color on the outside columns, although the saloon of the pillars was amber and black. Inside we were reminded of 'Hong Kong' murals.

"Communication yet privacy, shelter yet a grand view, simple lines yet spectacular stateliness all combine to make us see for ourselves that the Palace of Knossos was over 3,000 years ago one of the finest buildings ever known in an incomparably picturesque surrounding.

"Unlike Egypt and the existing Greek world, here was architecture dedicated quite realistically to the service and joy of man."

Alexandra II (age 8) reports in her diary:

"Mommy loves the writer Nikos Kazantzakis and he was born and buried in Crete."

I suppose in response, the mother Alexandra I says:

"One of the most moving things to me about being on the Island of Crete was to fill myself with thoughts of Nikos Kazantzakis. Crete is where he was born in 1883 and where he was buried in 1957. The years between he spent adoring Crete, Greece, and gave, through his writing, feelings, sensitivities, colors and a spirit we would not be familiar with without his passion and compassion. I was first introduced to him by my friend Tony Lykiardopulo in 1956 and I find each time I reread one of his books a part of me is stirred. I discover something new inside me which I needed help in understanding. His *Zorba* sees everything every day as if for the first time. Kazantzakis says of himself in his novel *Zorba*:

'While experiencing happiness, we have difficulty in being *conscious* of it. Only when the happiness is past and we look back on it do we suddenly realize—sometimes with astonishment—how happy we had been. But on this Cretan coast I was experiencing happiness and knew I was happy.'

"Zorba was everything Nikos wasn't and wanted to be—not fully but in spirit. I feel the depths of this great mystery, I feel Kazantzakis gave a gift as great as he was. Every pore of his being opened up for us so we could gain knowledge, understanding and appreciation of the Greek spirit, place and people, past and present and beyond. Nikos Kazantzakis, bless you. Thank you. I know you suffered and I know you lived your journey deeply. You may have not made my journey known in full to me or easier, you have helped me to understand how many paths there are now and how much traveling there can be in one lifetime toward that high goal, that high place."

Alexandra II (age 8): "Santorini used to be round but a gigantic volcanic eruption cut it in half, one part fell into the sea forever! Now there is a cliff one-thousand feet straight up. We landed there in a small fishing boat. We took a donkey ride up to the top of the hill while all the way up I was saying how mean it was for the donkey to spend his time taking fat heavy people up with no rest! One thousand feet! Well, we got up the hill, went shopping and had some ice cream and walked down. When we got down, I looked all the way up at the white houses."

Peter (father): "Sea Voyage to Santorini (Thera). Suddenly our boat entered a blue-green gulf and we were flat up against a menacing cliff rising straight up 1,000 feet from a tiny port. At the top peeping over was a white string of houses, churches, shops and the proud Hotel Atlantis. The earthquake of 1450 B.C. was an unparalleled catastrophe, devastating neighboring islands as well as destroying the first flower of the Minoan Empire in Crete 70 miles away (when the volcano exploded, the middle of the island sank; the sea rushed in, to be spurted out in a historic tidal wave across the whole Aegean Sea)."

"In 1967 archeologists dug into a bronze-age town on Santorini of 30,000 souls where three-story buildings and houses were found paralyzed in lava ash before the final explosion. Found within were extraordinary frescoes of plants, birds, people, fish—and antelopes and apes. Experts think these frescoes surpass all those of the Mediterranean including Egypt.

"The island is officially Thira (Thera), mostly known as Santorini, from its patroness, St. Irene of Thessalonika."

"Typical Greek mythology. 'Delos is the birthplace of the twins Apollo and Artemis, whose mother, Leto, was relentlessly pursued by the serpent Python, by the order of Hera, the jealous wife of Zeus, by whom she was pregnant.'

"And what we missed because of rough sea weather . . . *Delos* . . . One tree and eight beds—(at Xenia Hotel), a sacred place."

Nathaniel (age 14): "Arriving in Mykonos was exciting—we had heard so much about it. We anchored in a little harbor and took a tender to shore where buses were waiting to take us away to the town. Buses were slow to move and people got uptight but I always try to keep my cool on vacation. What's the rush? As my dad always says: 'You don't have to rush because we aren't going to the theater.'

"Mykonos was even more beautiful than we had hoped. Buildings so white you have to blink or turn away if you look at them too long. We wandered down to the wharf and then back again, up an alley and got thoroughly lost. Somehow we found our way back. We sat and had a

Coke and then decided we would go up and see the 'windmill hill' so we asked a few navigational questions and headed up. As we came to forks in the street it was a complete guessing game but we saw them and I led the troop on to the windmills, just waiting to have the company of five tourists at 9:00 in the morning.

"They were old and only one was working and it was making a real noise about it: squeaking and creaking as if to say that it was too old for this kind of work."

Alexandra II (age 8): "Mykonos is my best island—I love it! I saw the windmills. We had lunch by the water. We passed a few bakeries. We bought a model of the windmill. Here's a picture [set in her diary]"

Alexandra I (mother): "Walking through the maze of narrow whitewashed streets, getting lost in the labyrinth of bright dazzling light reflected against the blue-white light is the charm of Mykonos. Walking up to the hill of windmills with their white triangular sails and seeing them spinning around in the summer winds is a joy.

"We sat at an open cafe on the waterfront and watched the people. Mykonos wasn't crowded at all for an August Sunday. Our lunch was on the waterfront and we had shrimp, eggplant salad and vine leaves. It was earthy and beautiful. We hopped down another street for our Greek salad and our first taste of Retsina. I would drink Retsina again only if I were dying and was told this potion was my only help for a few more moments of life. There is nothing enjoyable about the taste of turpentine to my palate. Henry Miller drank it when he was in Greece in the early '40s but cautioned to drink it with a full meal of lamb and eggplant and bread."

Brooke (age 5): "No Delos—too windy. We walked around the harbor, saw the boats and shops. We bought a lot of colorful worry beads, walked around the narrow streets with the sunny glare. White buildings."

Nathaniel (age 14): "As we walked up we noticed a very nice restaurant that had a delicious Greek menu written on a wooden plaque. We sat and waited for service. We attracted attention and got some lunch—fresh shrimp with no formaldehyde and roasted chicken and spit-grilled lamb. What a meal, with a salad of dark red tomatoes and Greek olives.

"We moved on for our dessert at a neighboring restaurant so we could see and feel more. We ordered three watermelons and one bottle of white wine. My dad wasn't particular in Greece. He bought us delicious watermelon and a bottle of Retsina which is a wine with retsin in it and it tastes like old sneakers. We all read that it was terrible but now we know it is terrible.

"We moved on and passed a bakery where a man was making bread. We smelled the sweet aroma and poked our heads into the small shop but after a second of heaven the old bakerman yelled: 'No bread, No bread!' We retreated—walking back the way we came and had ice cream for three in a small café out on the waterfront. We sat in front of brightly colored fishing boats, people passing by and thinking of the days to come."

Alexandra I (mother): "Nathaniel had an urge, a deep driving urge to hit the water as he does now as I write. In fact, Nathaniel is a fish. We are about to see him plunge into the sea. Zorba dances; Nathaniel swims."

Brooke (age 5): "There was a restaurant on the beach where we had dinner. We had Moussaka and it was yum.

"We found a taxi to go back to the boat. I was tired and was glad I didn't have to walk because the last bus had left the beach."

Nathaniel (age 14): "The beach was pleasant and there was a blue sky and a warm sun to go with it.

"We swam in the clearest water I've ever been in, water skiied and sunbathed until 5 or 6 when we dressed and ate a snack of Moussaka which is a pie with meat and eggplant and a crusty topping. I prodded everyone on so we could make the 7:00 tender back to the ship. We started back and by chance a taxi came by and we flagged it down and said Stella Oceanis "Eclaristow" (which means 'Thank you'). We made it as it was taking off and I was glad because if we didn't we would have to wait an hour till the next one left. On the tender were my Spanish friends who spoke little English but had a lot of friendship to give."

After coming back through Athens we took an airplane for the trip to the Greek Island of Corfu.

Brooke (age 5): "Plane trip to Corfu—we're here? It was only a minute. Snap your fingers and we're here!"

Peter (father): "A swing to the northwest from Aegean to Ionian there is a special place near the heel of Italy but separated absolutely from brooding Albania—Corfu, an emerald scimitar surrounded by translucent seas and brilliant light, flushed with constantly changing colors of mother-of-pearl. I found this idyllic island (favorite of Lawrence Durrell) smelling of watermelon, cool and freshly cut.

"Two quotes from Lawrence Durrell:

(1) 'Waves of the invading East reached as far as the island; burst into these valleys and groves. [Corfu] stands as boundary stone in the history of Turkish conquest for it did not reach further. Here it broke and fell, and the key to the Adriatic was held firm by the Venetians.'

(2) 'The cypresses lining the road are perhaps the most ancient on the Island; their plumes are almost black, and near the ground are powdered by the fine golden summer dust.' "

"After release from its benign protectorate about a hundred years ago there is, in my opinion, by now nothing really left of the British influence other than perhaps cricket and marmalade.

"Corfu is an isle that has seduced not only the Durrell family—but also Ulysses, Nero, Cato, Julius Caesar, Napoleon, King Paul II, King Farouk, Henry Miller and Richard the Lionhearted—seems everybody *likes* it!"

Alexandra I (mother): "Lawrence and Gerald Durrell say this island is flawless. For years I've dreamed about coming here—not for a boat stopover but to take a house, unpack and, at least until a reasonable length of time has slipped by unhurried, to be. To be, to live in Corfu: my fantasy.

"I hear nothing but the sea which is drowning out the buzz of insects and the slight chirping of birds. Evening is here in a soft transition. The sun fades taking the blue. The sky and water have a mist and pale quality—a softness in preparation for eventual darkness and rest.

"We have been blessed with a moon for our entire stay in Greece. I am afraid tonight we will have to remember what the glow was like all these nights we dined with the moon glowing the darkened sea in a dazzling shimmer of diamonds moving, breathing, living with us each night. We saw the razor-thin new moon, like a scimitar the Greeks use to cut ground cover, when we were in Athens so we could see the pale pink cast of the pentelic white marble of the buildings on the Acropolis come alive by this light and each island we went to—each evening on board looking at the flickering Aegean Sea we were followed by this expanding circle. Now we must remember the moon as it was. I will create it in my mind until we leave." Brooke was particularly fond of the bungalow with its feet in the water at a place called Miramar where we lived next to the garden of the inn. She writes:

"Our bungalow is really nice because it is on the water and I always go down the path by the water to the nice man in the shop. There is a pool table by the lobby and there are ping-pong tables by the snack bar.

"Peter and Mommy brought us masks and flippers so I can see all the fish and shells. The water is really clear and there is a sandy bottom."

Peter (father): "Water Colors—Aegean and Ionian Seas. Deep throbbing emerald; laser nitric green; a sea of turquoise; sapphire at noon; golden pretzels of fractured sunlight dazzling the sandy bottom of the shore through prisms of pure water.

"Greek summer climate: 70–90 but without the humidity of the Caribbean or Bermuda.

"Corfu: an island of eternal Spring.

"Lush green island bathed in lilac light, washed by seas of emerald blue; shaded from piercing sun by battalions of gnarled olive trees, centuries old. Across is Albania and mainland Greece—a backdrop in stunning contrast to Corfu: barren, brooding and dark."

Alexandra I (mother): "This literal paradise, this isolated far-away island, lush and dripping with a flow of nature, surrounded by the Ionian Sea which strokes the shore in rhythmic pulsebeats is extraordinarily beautiful. I'm here living in a house a few yards from this moving film of sky and water. Our bed faces the sea and the only thing that separates me from a perfect canvas of sea and heaven is occasionally my toes get in the way."

Brooke (age 5): "We have flippers and a mask and all go in the water for family swims. I can swim underwater a long time."

Alexandra I (mother): "For days I've felt intimidated even to attempt to describe this setting. I have a friend in Connecticut who is a writer. He's told me on many occasions that when something is close to perfect it becomes more difficult to describe than something you can pick away at and illustrate the flaws.

"There are no imperfections here, and because of this and possibly the drugged feeling I have from being inside this natural harmony and spiritual home, my senses are more finely tuned to feel every ripple, every breeze, every color change, a bee, a fish and the sky.

"This island has a spirit of place, as Lawrence Durrell would say. Corfu is life seen through a looking glass where every mirror of beauty, all the flowering fruit trees, juicy figs, dignified olive trees, arrogant shafts of cypress, lush greens, contrasting gently against this kaleidoscope of seafoam blues, greens, purples and powder-soft blue sky would be seen through unscratched lens, dust free, in focus with lighting brighter and clearer and sunnier, happier than any you've ever experienced."

•   •   •

Corfu's elegant architecture is Venetian. Proud slim shuttered houses hug each other in a pleasing jumble along narrow alleys, with striking colonnades running along them. A fine mixture of Greek and Bermudian colors abound—rose, Spanish melon, sienna, umber, pistachio, tawny yellow, all set off in style with light-headed roccoco grill-work and balconies sufficient perhaps for a small cat. This classic town surrounds with generosity the largest square in Europe—the magnificent Spianada, protected by two soldier-boy forts reminiscent of Rhodes to the East at the other end of the Greek world.

Peter's (father) diary entry: "Back to our house—one night after dinner of Moussaka and Souvlaki, across the black of the sea we were startled by seven glaring lights several miles off the southeast coast toward Albania and mainland Greece. The night and sea were still; and the fat moon was reluctant to rise. From fishing boats huge carbide flares lure fish to the nets. We discussed among ourselves the morality of attracting fish to their doom at night by artificial lights. Brookie pondered this problem for a moment. 'I think it is unfair—I think it is unfair—especially for the fishes . . . ' "

My diary has notes on the old Corfu downtown area of Kerkyra, Corfu's capital:

"Weathered plaster of the 18th Century houses, allowed to go cracked umber, yet shuttered and regal. Wash out on the line, sometimes all across the narrow street. By observing the laundry out to dry each occupant of the dwelling is revealed. Even the most modest housing has in the windows balconies and niches, pots of geraniums, impatiens or greens. Pounding light floods the darkest spaces. Children play, men and women sell, trade and craft leather, wood and stone.

"*Aegli* is a spirited restaurant under the colonnades: typically good in the delicious dishes of the Island. You cannot help marvelling at the tomatoes, aubergine, fruit and random service that extends down and up the colonnades and waiters dodging traffic across the street to the esplanade. These facile waiters, alert and resourceful, full of bravado and not beyond serving you while at the same time nudging and addressing a passing blonde girl, who circles back on the opposite side."

Alexandra II (age 8) said in her diary: "I love Corfu with fresh air and narrow streets and beautiful flowers. One day we went into town and went into a bakery shop. We saw beautiful pastries. We asked what was what and found one we liked: it was an apple pastry. It was hot—and well I just can't spit the words out—well, it was super duper! Then we had lunch and a beautiful day."

Then these entries:

Alexandra I (mother): "Alexandra II and Brookie are in the water now with their flippers and masks. They have found a huge six foot log which is 'their boat' and they are entranced. The water is soft pale green. The yellow sand below has wavy ripples two inches apart and feels like cushions as you hop about underwater."

Brooke (age 5): "My sister lost her bikini bottom and Mommy offered a reward of ten drachma. I ran to go find the bathing suit before lunch because I wanted to win that Greek money. I found the bathing suit near the old room we used to stay in. I was so happy. I ran to Mommy's arms smiling all the way."

Alexandra I (mother): "I am lounging at the edge of the water. Across from me is Albania to the northeast and Greece to the southeast about 18–20 miles away. There is a mountain as sandy and dry as the pyramids in Giza and looks as though Brookie had gotten her watering can and rounded all the sharp edges. Across this living sea of blues bathed in mysterious light is a barren rocky land.

"Here in eyesight is a thick healthy hedge of morning glories which are strong peacock blue in the morning and fade to lavender blue in the afternoon as they prepare to close for the evening.

"Under all the olive trees is a ground cover called 'Aphrodite's Hair' which is singularly pea-pod in shape and reaches out toward the water and sun.

"At the north end of our house is a garden filled with yellow, orange, pink, purple and red zinnias and 'Astrickia' (small stars) with their lacy-thin petals in pinks and purples with yellow happy faces. We have fresh flowers in our rooms, even the bathrooms. The girls are in special charge of picking flowers and changing the water each day."

Brooke (age 5): "The flowers are pretty in Corfu. I picked up a flower on this page and pressed it. Pink, purple and yellow orange—all different colors. I pick them from the garden and put them in the bungalow."

Alexandra II (age 8): "Corfu is very green. We have a house which is over the water. We had a garden! We watched the sunset! It was wonderful! But then the day came when we had to travel on home . . . "

Alexandra I (mother): "On the west side of our house we have a tangerine tree, lemon trees with white blossoms, one which bears 'ugly' type fruit, orange trees, prune trees, a peach tree, and down the path leading to our house, which is the furthest away from people of all the houses on the water here, there is a pale pink oleander with fine pinwheel leaves and peppermint centers, darker pink oleanders, jasmine, fan palm, bamboo, hibiscus.

"The middle of our tawny yellow house is open to the sky and has been given over to a regal olive tree, proudly there for five hundred years. Each bedroom looks directly east over the Ionian Sea with a columned terrace in front of sienna shutters.

"On this side of the island there are pebbles instead

of sand at the water's edge. Despite love for the white sandy beaches of the Caribbean I find these smooth egg-shaped stones fascinating. Alexandra II and Brooke have made a collection of tile chips, fitting them together like a mosaic—most discovered underwater or washed ashore. Corfiot workmen throw them to sea when they are finished tiling a bathroom! Colored treasures under water.

"From prior trips to Greece I have brought back tiny smooth pebbles and put them in silver cigarette boxes to be rubbed in hand and examined. Each one demands special attention. Yesterday Brooke found a stone with a portrait of a cocker spaniel. A child's treasure.

"The second highest mountain on Corfu is Aghios Dimetrios and is about three miles south and swings like an arm east. We all see a lady lying down after a too-big lunch and her highest peak reaches up about 600 M (3'3" per meter).

"Because it is so clear I feel as though I could reach over and touch the mountain top but when I study it with binoculars I see in detail whole villages and fields of olive groves and the entire green curving blanket broken up in horizontal harmony by armies of marching postured cypress trees. Taller and more energetic than the bending twisted irregular olive trees. Cypress trees are definitely human—they are a whole lot more reserved and rigid than their neighbors.

"Olive trees spread out their trunks from the roots up and grow in a freedom determined by the environment in which they were planted. The Venetians gave ten gold pieces to Corfiots who planted an olive grove of a hundred trees. Then there were over two million trees and today over three and a half million. When planted on a hill they grow toward the sea—light and air so they reach at all angles disregarding the purely vertical position of the cypress.

"The trunk of an olive tree is elephant-like with wrinkles and a grey leathery appearance—pitted with holes. When you drive through an olive grove you see the blue-green sea and sky beyond through many of the tree trunks which are opened as views from one side of the trunk through to the other.

"As I sit writing, the waves are folding over and over freshly bringing this salty clear water to my attention saying gently—come, come, swim.

"Small black olives are dropping from the tree right on me every few minutes as the wind moves their silver leaves. Olive leaves are small (about 1" to 1½" long on an average) and it appears to me they are always being twisted around by the wind. The tops of the leaves are actually a strong green color but it is the bottom which is pale and silver which gives the silver shimmer to the groves.

"When you find yourself in paradise where the air is so fresh and each breath is a sensory treat, all earthy, all good smells, all sweet, I found my appetite has increased. Afternoon tea by the sea tastes so much nicer out-of-doors with a sweet cake and jasmine in the air and the fruit trees. Swimming also gives me a wonderful hollow feeling so I emerge from underwater life to the warmth of the sun and smells of aubergine being fried in olive oil pressed from nearby trees. Olives drop black and ripe in November. Many people have nets beneath the trees to catch the ripen olives as they fall. I've heard stories that the branches are shaken and the ripe olives fall from the trees but I prefer to believe (especially on Corfu) it is the wind, patience of divine nature and perfect timing that drops these black teardrops from their branches.

"I am at my desk facing the water. There is a breeze flowing freshness from the front of our house where the fruit trees are to the back of the house. A few fishing boats pass by. In front of me is a Corfu pottery vase holding a few dozen bows of pink shooting star flowers, reaching in all directions. Their skinny bending petals look as if they were made of crêpe paper and cut into hundreds of strips. Jasmine is mixed in for fragrance and the palest pink-white blossom stands out against such a mass of pink. I always have fresh flowers on my writing desk wherever I am—one fresh flower is enough—even if it is a fallen blossom otherwise unappreciated."

＊＊   ＊＊   ＊＊

In Greece is to see everything reborn—fresh. Nothing is too big or too small to appreciate. Because the light is so perfect you can see 30 miles of coastline and from the same perspective see an olive tree above you and take one small branch and study each leaf and olive, glance at the soft aqua sea below and under the rippling quiver study the pebble candy beneath—pebbles all look delicious—caramels and nuggets and candy-coated almonds. People told us we were wasting our time and money taking children to the Mediterranean so young. To feel better, we repeated what the microbiologist René Dubos had said in a recent book, that "Practically all environmental impacts leave an imprint on the body and the mind. This imprint is likely to be almost irreversible, especially if it occurs early in life."

Near the end of our stay in Corfu by the water, Alexandra's diary entry shows:

"This is the belief I have had in my life and my work: we are formed and shaped by these exposures and experiences, good and bad, hollow or deep, rich or weak, beautiful or ugly, and all of these influences work together to create larger wholes, greater truths, knowledge, love.

"Everything counts. Every flower, every sunrise, every piece of marble, every song of a bird in the early morning, each ripple of the water reaching out to shore creates the character and the framework of our minds so we can then, with patience and feeling, use our entire being to create what is most real to us and grow to be the person we find through all these exposures and experiences.

"The day is slipping to dusk. Colors soften. Candy clouds slumber off Albania. Tomorrow at six we rise to fly to Athens, then home to New York. We've had tea and without the warmth of the sun we feel chill. Alexandra II and Brookie are sketching mountains. None of us wants to leave and disrupt this moment. This will be a memory. We want to extend and keep it alive."

As the diaries of the five of us wound down on our preparation for returning to New York, Alexandra I commented: "The only sadness about our trip ending is knowing that we know it can never be duplicated and in our quest for new experiences we won't even try to. This is the sadness—the page being turned and suddenly you realize that that was the last word in the book. That period ended your journey."

As we flew into New York, Alexandra II read us a passage from Henry Miller's *The Collosus of Mourussi*:

"Greece is what everybody knows, even *in absentia*, even as a child or as an idiot or as a not-yet-born. It is what you expect the earth to look like given a fair chance. It is the sublimal threshold of innocence. It stands, naked and fully revealed. It is not mysterious, or impenetrable. Not awesome. Not defiant. Not pretentious. It is made of earth, air, fire and water. It changes seasonally with harmonious undulating rhythms. It breathes, it beckons. It answers."

Memories of that family odyssey to the Greek Mediterranean stay with us. Our experience in the Greek Mediterranean expands, rather than contracts, as we alone and together "contemplate the essence of it."

–V–

BERMUDA WRITER'S WORKSHOP: PLEASURES IN READING AND WRITING IT DOWN

Several years ago two people sat on a terrace on the south shore of Bermuda facing the turquoise sea. One person started to relate an anecdotal experience about an earlier time on the island fifty years ago, when the other person put down her book, saying positively: "Why don't you write it down?"

So from then on we both began to "write it down"—from memories and deep wells of others' experiences and reflections. We discussed each other's progress, selection of books and papers, the quality of writing pads and the flow of colored inks in a variety of fountain pens.

Slowly, not unlike sculpturing and painting, the book or the article is shaped and, possibly one day accepted by a publisher. Few thrills approach the exhilaration caused by seeing your own work actually there—*printed* in a publication!

In this ordinary way the two of us fell into a happy pattern we call "the Writer's Workshop" which brings serendipitous pleasures in reading and in writing, sharpening our senses, increasing our joy of living—and doing it all in a relatively inexpensive and uncomplicated way, in a blessed environment of serenity and beauty, away from traffic, honk and crowd, fresh breezes sweeping the inspiring beaches of pink sand below us. Time is captured.

Not everyone will be lured into such a reading and writing scenario. Some spouses are keenly aloof to the other's tastes in literature and writing. James Joyce's wife Nora (Molly Bloom in *Ulysses*) refused to read his work, once saying, when fame came to her husband, "I don't know whether my husband is a genius or not, but he certainly has a dirty mind."

Variations are surely allowed on the theme of your Writer's Workshop. We have in the last few years settled joyfully into a pattern that suits us well and has penetrating psychic results. By working extra hours during the week in New York as a counsellor-at-law and interior designer, respectively, we arrange to fly to Bermuda each Friday morning, returning to work (with an hour saved) on the early Monday morning flight in time to arrive with our colleagues. With this schedule, our Writer's Workshop gives each of us three uninterrupted days for reading and writing—about twenty-seven pure hours of concentration, healthy sun and air and the refreshing excitement of creation.

We are invigorated and soothed by the timeless rhythms of the waves on the reef and shore and appreciate the smell of jasmine, the color of hibiscus and morning glory, and the sound of surf and wind.

While this program is essentially a summertime idyll, the concept of reading and writing in other places and at our home on Carnegie Hill goes on the year round.

More specifically, Writer's Workshop entails a few commitments and, yes, a little discipline, with a dash of advance work. During the week, in preparation, we gather thoughts about subjects and themes to be expressed, in what form—book, article or paper—sources of the proposed enterprise—rented library books, or own marked books and articles, and maybe earlier notebooks and diaries. From friends and book reviews, we've learned of relevant new materials or older books, often paperback classics of another age.

These resources constitute the water for our well. As food for the Workshop episode in mind, we bring it all, carefully suitcased, to the selected spirited Bermuda place, where we plunge into our endeavor together, allowing a welcome freedom from the angst of heavy labour and the yawning banalities of boredom and oppression. We are free as birds to stop or to go. The hairshirt notion fostered by sports writer Red Smith that to write we must be alone and miserable should be discarded as myth. The presence of your fellow Workshop reader-writer seems to exercise a gentle restraint on your urge from time to time to go off and do something else. Perseverance pays off as you see and feel accomplishment, not great literature, mind you, but something acceptable out of you, that when finally read to your co-worker (on a basis of tolerant interplay), you begin to appreciate, as Virginia Woolf did, the rhythm and song of writing and reading, just for the sheer pleasure of it. Reading out loud is beneficial and lets you stay in tune with the voice.

One day on the terrace, a strong fluff of wind took three written sheets off the table and down a fifty-foot coral cliff. Alexandra jumped up, descended to the beach, crawled precipitously up the cliffside until—mirable dictu—she rescued, unscathed, her precious papers of writing, tucking them safely in the top of her bathing suit. From then on she uses a clipboard!

The process, Samuel Johnson said, *is* the reality. The reading and the writing *is* the reality—not in an airless, messy office, glued to modern man's green-lighted computer terminal, but open and free on a terrace, the favorite pen moving across good bond paper, marked books and xeroxed papers readily available to your reach, a portable dictionary at your side. (No intelligent person knows how to spell, don't we agree?) Since the process is what life is about, there should be no anxiety about whether the product of your work will in fact be published. Emily Dickinson had only several poems published in her whole lifetime. We believe sincerely there is a book in almost every person alive. (The key word here is "alive.") Books are treasures, personal treasures. Winston Churchill urged us to pick them up, feel them, glance through, before reading them. Books become, quite intimately, extensions of ourselves. We grow with them. They are the library of our minds. Each day's experience is rescued from the commonplace and often rises to new insights and fresh perspectives.

It is, after all, not how long we live but rather the *quality* of our lives that gives us energy and joy. We are what we read. Reading and writing, in combination such as the Workshop idea, can compliment and enhance each other, as gracefully and symbiotically as love.

The rewards are not in heaven. That can wait. The rewards of reading and writing are here, available to all of us, everywhere, so we should endeavor to experiment with this excitement and happiness before it is too late for us and the time has gone aimlessly by.

So we suggest—when the spirit moves you— "*write it down!*"

–VI–

MIRIAM

Miriam always has been intuitive and singularly compassionate, like green-violet eyes filling with tears. It is her genetic nature. In earlier days Miriam was also athletic and graceful as a Mohawk. She could win foot races and shoot ocean waves faster than her two daughters and two sons—at least until they approached their late teens, and often then too.

If you had to characterize Miriam, mostly a dangerous practice, you'd have to say Miriam was an artist most of her life—in the true sense of the word. An artist who, seemingly without effort, could find color, texture and balance in proportions that live in the memory long after the time of her creation.

She was the youngest daughter of four, blessed one day with a baby brother who became her closest companion as a child. One day her brother at twelve ate roasted chestnuts from a Philadelphia street peddler and suddenly died of scarlet fever. This tragedy deeply affected Miriam and lived among her memories into her nineties. She said the saddest thing in life is to simply consider what might have been.

The Megargee family home in Philadelphia in the 1890's was run by a governess who, although purportedly French, teutonically dictated the daily household routine. Miriam's Father was at the office managing his paper mill, laboriously producing the finest writing paper, at racing creeks near Chestnut Hill which flowed down to the Schukyll River. The first American paper mill was founded by William Rittenhouse in what is now Fairmount Park. This paper, providing the Revolution and the founding of America with its paper, documents and the Continental Army's cartridge and gun wadding, her father insisted, was less superior than the smooth, strong rag paper Megargee Mills produced with 19th century chemical expertise. The rags, he said, made the difference.

When summer came the family took carriages out to the farm along the Main Line in Gladwyne. The house is now gone, yet you can see the footage of the foundation, the circular stone road up to the top of the hill, the great green sprawling oaks and elms, and down below a secluded glimpse of the farmer's cottage, outbuildings and the barn, now faded red in the morning sunlight. In this microcosm, Miriam and her brother found the mysterious subjects of life and nature that would somehow stay with her for almost a century of time.

One summer day at the family luncheon table at the farm, at the children's end of the table, the question was raised as to what was being served to them to eat. Miriam and her brother, who had a particular fondness for each of the chickens down at the barn, spontaneously looked at each other, and suddenly exclaimed—"Oh no!" They then blurted out together that at this lunch they were being served "Blackie," in the form of roast chicken. This broke up the midday meal and Miriam and her brother were sent to their rooms by the governess.

Straight east from Philadelphia was a summer place on the ocean called Chelsea, Atlantic City, a residential area removed from the excitement of salt water taffy and splintering boardwalks, hot dogs and pretzels with mustard. It was summer holidays in Chelsea that Miriam, in her teens, learned to swim in rough surfs, handle the riptides and sea pussies, know how to judge and manipulate the high rolling waves—and to ride them, without a board, for endless runs right up to the beach itself, high and dry. For these occasions she and her sisters wore the complete bathing suits, showing no skin, tight around the smallest waists, dark stockings and floppy caps that somehow would stay on amidst the waves.

Also vacationing in Chelsea was a Yale college student who disconcerted the array of bathers at the shore by methodically running up and down the beach in his bathing suit—dark trunk pants, horizontal blue-striped sleeveless top. They met during one of these energetic daily forays and she learned that this young man was apparently developing running speed and stamina for the college track team. Miriam fell into the run on the beach one day until he had to slow down and stop, as she showed sufficient vitality to overtake him. It would be the following spring at the Harvard stadium when he would break the intercollegiate half-mile record (1:54 seconds) as the speedy captain of the undefeated Yale team.

Miriam chose him for her own after a courtship of dancing and dining in Philadelphia and Chelsea. They were married in January, 1917, and were together, like swans, until his untimely death in 1946. He took Miriam to the mud-strewn milltown of New Kensington, Pa., to start his business career with the Aluminum Company of America. Its President was Arthur Vining Davis who, courting a lady whose daughter, Dorothy, George Brown was courting before he married Miriam, asked him one day in New Haven what he was going to do after graduation. He said he wasn't sure. A. V. Davis said, "Well, George, why don't you come to work for my company?" He knew then his career was made, receiving such an invitation from the chief executive officer. But he learned over several years that the president and the rookie employee in one of America's largest manufacturing companies were in two separate worlds.

He chose in a few years to take Miriam and their four children to New York to enter the brokerage business with his college roommate Francis Thorne. The twenties was a booming business atmosphere. Speculation by a large majority of people was creating a new age of stocks and bonds and accounts on margin of ten percent.

First on the south shore of Long Island and then in 1927 to Carnegie Hill, New York City, summering in Quogue, Long Island, Miriam and I—from the time I was three years old to seven—became companions in a daily round of repeated activities. In the old Ford Model A in Babylon we went to the Mom and Pop grocery store, to Mr. Farrara's fruit store, to the shoemaker, to the pharmacy, to the dressmaker on the edge of town, to the friendly hatted butcher—and I remember as a special treat to the local movie theater to see "Dawn Patrol." Miriam treated these visits as special occasions to converse and transact with special people. Dealings were never automatic or impersonal. She knew the owners quite well and dealt directly with them. The relationship would be effective and courteous or she would move on to another "little man." Supermarkets did not exist. If they had, I know we would have avoided them.

Miriam made the clothes for all her children when they were young—until the time came when they revolted. Every two weeks she was the barber for haircuts, victims sitting backwards in the bathroom on a toilet seat. With most of the children in school in the 1930s, Miriam began to paint with oils. First her subjects were cows, ducks, dogs, polo ponies, gardens and landscapes. She would always see to it that her companion with her, no matter how incompetent, would participate in the art work. A dab of paint here or there to encourage the blessing of creativity. She was instructed in her artistic endeavor by her second cousin, Edwin Megargee, a recognized painter of dogs and birds, and by a singular lady of strange demeanor, Miss Wilson, whose studio we'd visit up a flight on Madison Avenue just below the Westbury Hotel, while receiving her meticulous teaching techniques. Miss Wilson wore a splattered smock, spoke kindly in a gravelled voice, amazing me with her way of dangling a lighted Lucky Strike from her lips while jabbing her canvass abruptly, with a long, thin camel hair paint brush. "There, there, there," she'd grumble to herself, until finally content with the desired image.

Miriam also loved the creative comfort of needle-work—nurtured by her infinite patience and resolution. I watched her do the backs and seats of all the dining room chairs in rich colored green and gold and black wools, depicting the Brown family crest—a swan about to rise, or about to fall.

Her tour de force was to paint early Chinese mandarin family scenes on all the walls of the dining room, which took months. My father became concerned. "Miriam, don't you think you should be painting these scenes on canvas so they can be removed?" She kept on working, finally replying: "It will be all right. I'm not going anywhere."

Miriam became a veritable factory, turning out handpainted ducks, wooden cigarette boxes with scenes of Old Westbury, large lacquered screens depicting flower bouquets and romantic landscapes of Old England. Her needlework was turned out like the Sorcerer's Apprentice's buckets of water. This of course was during the Depression and at a time when she also collected string and was never known to throw anything away.

One day Miriam announced she was going to do a 4½-inch wide bell pull, about six feet long, in grand colors in regular and petitpoint stitch. What was the scene to be for the bell pull?, we asked. "It will be a scene showing the flight of male and female ducks across a beautiful blue sky." There was a skeptical pause at this point, eyes rolling upward, because we realized the narrow tie of a bell pull could not take the horizontal flight of ducks. But she completed her work in a few weeks. It is, I think, an ingenious work of art—which I have in my office—of majestic mallards rising felicitously from a marsh, upward, upward into an early morning sky. She did it.

Miriam and her husband always had a tacit understanding—that they loved each other and that their first priority was their family. There was never any disagreement about that. These were for their lives forever, their touchstones. At the same time it was evident, quite often to some—the snob, the pretentious social climber, the commercial phony, the fake personality, that Miriam's kind and generous personality had the limits of an envelope. Personal tolerance with the wicked and cheat would go just so far. She had no college or graduate study, simply, a finishing up at Miss Irwin's School and Shipley's in Philadelphia. Her intuition about people and behavior were keen, honed, I think, by curiosity, patient observation and imagination. She never complained. She was an unsuspecting judge of character, seldom reversed.

Miriam told me many things, many ideas, some almost clairvoyant, that I accepted on faith at a young age, to discover later had no scientific accuracy or authority— only years later to find that these theories and notions had been recently "discovered" in laborious testings, experiments and surveys. She believed, for example, that we should eat a little of everything because we'd never know until too late which particular ingredient was necessary to save our health if not our life.

From the earliest days on the Chelsea beaches she never exposed her face or her body to the rays of the sun although even then it was thought sexy to be tan. She felt the sun was artificial and in large doses could serve to age the skin, lending a depressed and forlorn look to a person, who certainly was seeking the opposite. She took care of her own fingernails in a natural way. She loved cold cream and would use it generously at night time. She understood the value of an active, physical life. Nothing excessive such as lifting or moving furniture, but rather gentle, graceful movements about. Getting up and down. Walking to engagements, rather than always driving. She was not ashamed to keep regular hours and order fruits and salads and fresh vegetables every day. She ate fish regularly when it was for most people only a Friday ritual. It sounds so banal were it not so successful—she always went to the market herself to pick out what would be delivered for her family table. She was not afraid, socially, to go to bed early, urge others to do so too, and be up at dawn every day, to see that everyone had breakfast. I remember not one single day when she was not there to see us fed and safely off to school on time. She will not receive the Pulitzer Prize for saying for over half a century "Breakfast is the most important meal of the day."

The artist in her was neither temperamental nor pretentious. Her response to beauty and proportion was quite natural. As if it had always been this way, and why not? A felicitous nonchalance. She adored perfume bottles such as Shalimar, going so far as to buy them for the design and later perhaps coming to like the perfume itself. Fine paper in colorful patterns "drove her crazy" with appreciation. She would save these items for endless periods of time. Only a physical move or a fire would separate her from her treasures assuredly of no monetary value.

Most of all she loved the look of jewelry, all her life, with a passion. Not for its dollar value such as at a Park-Bernet auction but because of what the jewelry said to her as she gazed on its special magic. Rubies, emeralds, pearls of all kinds, stones I've never heard of, some considered by her friends as a bit gaudy—really, Miriam, it's not done, my dear. A pastime for Miriam was an afternoon at the old de Settles Jewelry Shop on Madison Avenue. Such looking, exchanging, considering, the conversation revolving around buying, remodeling, reshaping, putting in a circle of small diamonds, resetting and restringing.

Some years ago I introduced Miriam to Alexandra. Miriam was not always cordial or effusive with young ladies I introduced to her when she was still living on the 12th floor of an apartment on 78th Street and Park Avenue in the 1970s. One Sunday we picked her up and took her to the church on 90th Street she had been attending since the Sunday it opened on Easter Day, 1929. Her daughters

Harriett and Barbara had been married there after World War II. We returned to her apartment for lunch. Sitting on a sofa, Miriam took Alexandra's hands in hers. "You have lovely hands," she said, for they had in several weeks become fast friends. "But dear Alexandra, these hands of yours are lonely. They need some colorful friendly stones." She then went down the hall to her safe, the size of a small crate, spun the combination with the deftness of Willie Sutton and returned with fishermen fly-bait-lure plastic boxes. Around the boxes were rubber bands and string. Miriam proceeded to remove the bindings, revealing in each section of the boxes incredible numbers of brilliant stones of all colors, sizes and shapes, some mounted on handmade gold settings.

Alexandra could not believe what she was seeing. Miriam urged her to select a ring of her choice. After some hesitancy, Alexandra picked an emerald stone the size of a grape with a gold setting. Miriam put it on her finger and said: "That is very nice, but it still looks lonely on your finger. I think you should pick another to go with it!" More insisting. So Alexandra picked a companion star sapphire stone set in a gold mounting—the two now glistening together magically. "Well, that's better," Miriam said. "Now we can go in to lunch. I feel so much better. I hope you do!"

When father had died prematurely in 1946, Miriam was only 49, still slim, with beautiful long raven hair. Her light complexion, freed of the burn of the sun, was perfect. Her sadness nonetheless was overwhelming. She had lost her companion and her love. She told me her life was over and she would just await her end. That was 43 years ago. The sentiment has not changed much. About fifteen years ago she met a widower who lived nearby on the upper East Side named Walter, a good-natured, strong and handsome man of Scots ancestry. Friends asked Miriam where had she met her attentive and charming Walter. "Walter and I met at the Opera," Miriam would say. Later I found out that Miriam and Walter met one bright Spring day on the second park bench in from the entrance to Central Park at 72nd Street and Fifth Avenue.

Walter is still charming at 105 years of age, living across the street from us at 1192 Park Avenue on Carnegie Hill. When he was 100 he gave a luncheon at the Colony Club for his family and invited us too. This was a momentous occasion for a great Scot and for us. What I remember the most, I think, is that Walter got up, responding to exuberant toasts, to tell us, so poignantly, what it was like to live and love in New York City in the 1890s.

The draw of your original home roots are more powerful than we sometimes think. Miriam found her Park Avenue apartment more of a burden than she cared for and decided to go back to the Philadelphia Main Line area in which she grew up—the house, the trees, the changing seasons, the farm in Gladwynn explored so marvellously with her brother. So she retired down to Philadelphia, about eleven years ago, promising, promising to keep in the closest touch with her family and with Walter.

One day I was visiting her at her Dunwoody apartment, near Bryn Mawr, furnished with her own things, paintings and memories. There was a wonderful letter from Walter on her bureau, opened and read, received several weeks previously. "Well, this is nice, a letter from Walter," I said. "Are you going to write him a letter back today?" Miriam looked at me with her green-violet eyes, now misted with grey. "You know, Peter, I just don't have the time." When she told me that I suddenly recollected a conversation after my father, her husband, died forty years ago. She would be lonely, wouldn't she, after all those years together? "Whenever you really love someone," she replied slowly, "you are never alone."

On Carnegie Hill in the 1930s I remember when we were all together as a family—never thinking for a moment it would not always go on the same way. Miriam never failed to be there at the front door of the apartment when my father came home from Wall Street. She had bathed, had on a fresh dress, a dab of Shalimar perfume behind each ear, a smile and a kiss—which we children frankly thought was ridiculous. When we said so to her, she shook her head, eyes flashing. "No, I think if I weren't here for him when he comes home from a hard day, someone else would be . . . "

When I last remember talking to Miriam in a garden seat at Dunwoody, I asked her about father. What were her thoughts after all these years and the end drawing near? She lifted her head and looked out at the oaks and the elms, across to the hill. "Whenever you think of someone, he is never dead. That's what memory can do for us."

–VII–

CONTINUITY OF HAPPINESS

In what seems to be, for all of us, a short and turbulent life, *continuity* of anything—especially happiness—becomes paramount. Unconsciously perhaps, we seek happiness every day, wherever we happen to be and whatever we happen to be doing. For most people, happiness is a goal.

America was declared independent in 1776 with Thomas Jefferson's ringing phrase—every person's right to pursue happiness. This aspiration cradled the launch of a vibrant nation, the most risky experiment ever devised. This amazing concept, of happiness as a social goal once openly expressed, produced a Constitution of equity and order lasting longer than any other in world history.

The great philosopher Aristotle taught his students in Greece in the fourth century B.C. that our task as human beings is to achieve the "highest human good" which, he forcefully asserted, is happiness. Aristotle defined happiness as an "activity of the soul" in accordance with virtue. But to find happiness, he instructed, we must first find the habitat in which to pursue happiness, naturally a place conducive, indeed ripe with affirmation, to allow such joy and tranquillity. This sublime state of mind is not of course a moment's experience, a fix on the spot, rather an episode of continued euphoria lodged within us. In today's world of discord, terrorism, drugs, poverty and sorrow, to what place in the name of Heaven would Aristotle lead us to find continuity of happiness?

My grandparents came to Bermuda on their honeymoon in the 19th century on a schooner out of Philadelphia. They reported their happiness derived from these idyllic islands to all who would listen, for they believed sincerely that they had discovered, as 17th century Juan Bermudez and other settlers also discovered, a place of extraordinary spirit, climate and beauty—the most northern coral islands washed by the warmth of the Gulf Stream, alive with birds and fish and graced with cerulean skies and ocean waters startling turquoise, as if lapis lazuli were crushed by Greek gods into aqua marine.

"Living close to the sea is good for your head," says Beach Boy Brian Wilson, whose house overlooks California's Santa Monica Bay. "You're living at the foot of eternity, and it gives you perspective."

Bermuda is a jewelled string of islands which give you magnificent perspective, only 500 miles from the North Carolina coast, where residents and visitors can do their own experiment with continuity, leading to happiness and those poignant memories of felicitous things that somehow make our lives worthwhile. With our foot in eternity we can slip these memories into the banks of our minds and run them like videos at later times for solace and for recall.

I first came to Bermuda in 1937 to a small cottage on the south shore. This occasion of observation and contemplation stays with me now. My father, mother, sisters, brother and cousin were here too, and they form a continuous skein of tumbling pleasant memories. They continued at times of celebration and of play to return to Bermuda—to various locations but always by the sea, because, by some geographical magic, all Bermuda places are "by the sea."

My wife Alexandra and I came to Bermuda on our honeymoon, to a cottage appropriately named "Morning Glory," high on a green hill overlooking the deep blue ocean. We return regularly to savor the continuity and the opportunity to pursue happiness. My wife's mother and father came to Bermuda's dulcet Somerset on their honeymoon.

Starting years ago we followed our instinct and began to bring our children down for a blessed holiday and a moment's peace. We find the same generous spirit of the people, the same well kept gardens and lawns, pastel coral houses, the same cheerful atmosphere and remarkable good will. The place literally invites us to enjoy and be happy. It is hard to grouch or complain. Where else but in Bermuda will a taxi driver (Mr. Ball this weekend) stop his cab on the way from the airport to point out to his passengers the sight of aqua-mint parrot fish feeding in a cove of Smith Bay?

We see in the ambiance of Bermuda a generational ritual rare in modern society. Grandparents choose to bring grandchildren to Bermuda where they are introduced to healthy outdoor pleasures the grandparents themselves discovered years ago. No neon signs, no garbage dumps, no developer's bulldozers or beaches strewn with plastic mar the memories of earlier days. (In Bermuda the people have made no shortsighted commercial rush to have this place look and feel like Cannes, Atlantic City, Coney Island or

Nassau. The whole of Bermuda is enchanting. Even the drive to and from the airport is refreshing, beautiful and clean.)

One of the oldest cottages on the south shore, known worldwide for its broad pink sands and pure gentle surf, is called "Crow's Nest." With different combinations of family, we have come there eagerly and lovingly for years. The cottage sits proudly in Paget on the hills above the coral cliffs descending to the sea. There was always the vibrant changes of weather, sometimes in an hour, the presence of two hungry cats, the enticing aroma of coffee and bacon at breakfast time, cooked with an option of French toast, by a humming lady whose name continues to be Viola. After even a three-year absence at "Crow's Nest" you would still receive a warm greeting from Viola. Within the cottage, carefully preserved by a series of reverent visitors, are several leather bound albums in which the honest inscriptions of those who come and go have been faithfully subscribed, sometimes with children's art work and a pressed flower.

Here is revealed, perhaps unconsciously, the glorious continuity of the good times together. The incomparable continuity of family and friends, bound together for those brief moments of time in a place that draws us back again and again. The books still there today go back to the 1930's. I read of the families who come for the first time from St. Louis, from Atlanta, from Cleveland, Portland, Baltimore, London, Boston, Bryn Mawr and San Francisco.

Weather in a beach-oriented existence is a constant topic. It is good. It is bad. Viola is praised for her French toast. The cats were not back this year. The family picnic at Horseshoe Bay. The time together is put down as joyous, memorable. Then at the end, over and over, "We'll be back next year."

•   •   •

So, Aristotle told us, continuity of happiness is the best, the finest, "the most pleasurable of all." There is an ancient inscription at the entrance of the temple of Leto at Delos in the Aegean suggesting:
"Justice is loveliest, and health is best
But sweetest to obtain is heart's desire."

–VIII–

LETTER TO JULIA

Dear Julia:

You are my first grandchild. Almost three years old by now. Already I'm proud of you for your spirited love of life and marvelous love of parties. You also have a delicious knack of speaking your mind. When I say, "Come over here, Julia, and let me hug you," you say, your eyes emphatic, "NO!"

So today I thought I'd write you a letter telling you a little impressionistic story about where you came from. Not that this is essential or even important. Just out of curiosity, looking back once in a while at your ancestors can provide a clue or two, not any less credible I suppose than Nancy Reagan's astrology.

First, a few words of caution. America hates ancestor worship. It is unbecoming, unless in some group where everyone has an ancestor or two to worship. To put it lightly, America is a "New World"—only a few hundred years old. We are all immigrants here and in coming from distant lands, few brought genealogical records of who is who, when. Most of us came here with a carpetbag, if that.

One recent day it occurred to me, out of the blue, that every single person you will ever meet has ancestry going back—I swear it—to the beginning of time! You don't have to have a precious genealogical chart to prove that. If your father, grandfather or grandmother was first-rate, the chances are good that some of the gimp he or she possessed will show in you naturally, not because you strive for it but in spite of all you can do to escape. Also, we have to remember to keep a weather eye, as my grandfather John A. S. Brown told me, on the third and fourth generation ancestors, for one might be heralded as "honest" and "distinguished" and another might have been a "smuggler" or a "horse thief." Remember always that the passengers who came to America on the first well-known boat, The Mayflower, were not first-cabin or travelling POSH (port out, starboard home). Some may have deserted after landing the cargo. Or disappeared after eating a turkey or two.

One day at Plymouth, Massachusetts I actually went aboard an exact replica of The Mayflower and was amazed at the small size of the cabin. As big as a bathroom. I wondered how in the world these few intrepid passengers could have endured the passage over from Plymouth, England.

For every ancestor you ever had who received honorable mention in battle, I don't doubt that at least four feigned death and departed after nightfall.

In the balmy days of the Sun King, Louis XIV, in France in the 18th century there was a brilliant officer at the Court, highly regarded by the king. A jealous noble approached the officer at Versailles and acidly said: "You have no background. You have no lineage. You have no ancestors *like I do!*" The officer paused a moment and then looking at the agitated noble in the eye, cooly replied: "Yes, but you see, sire—*I am an ancestor.*"

So there is good reason for passing over our curious backward glance and saying "never mind about our progenitors, let's pay our bills and not talk so much."

Without your saying "NO!" I'd like to sketch a few lines for you about some of your forebears on my side of the family, that is, your sweet mother, Blair Tillyer Brown Hoyt, simply because I'm more familiar with these persons. This will include brief references—all absolutely true, of course—to my father's and mother's ancestors, namely Browns, de Rapalyées, Estabrooks, Willards, and Megargees and Johnsons on my mother's side. When you are older, and you feel like it, you can fill in my gaps, flesh out the picture on your paternal side and correct errors in my account. Always keep in mind what King Solomon warned us. "All is vanity and blowing in the wind."

•   •   •

The first Brown family member to come to America was Thomas Browne, baptized in 1605 at the handsome church of St. Peter and St. Paul in Lavenham, Suffolk, England, a few miles northeast of London. The town was prosperous from the wool trade and even today the church with its square stone tower is beautiful, its lanes and byways now bicycled by tourists from all over the world. Thomas Browne was born in Bury St. Edmunds, as carefully recorded in the Middlesex probate registry. In 1637 Thomas and his brother Edmund came to America and were, for there were few people here, the original proprietors of Sudbury, Massachusetts. Edmund became the first minister of Sudbury.

The Browns and the Estabrooks were for generations ministerial families—that is, they served the church as clergy and otherwise as lay servants of the church as wardens and vestrymen for some ten generations in our country. It was in the nature of duty never discussed, and from what I gather has been very satisfying.

Several years ago I was gently escorted through the ancient and sacred Forbidden City in Beijing, China, one sunny afternoon by a young Chinese lady. We had just enjoyed a grand luncheon banquet at the summer palace of the last empress, adjacent to a lovely lake. She described, with great enthusiasm and precision, the history of the ancient buildings, temples and shrines. This one was 13th Century; this was 11th Century; This, 10th Century! I was awed by the aura of the past, evident in such splendor and symmetry. As we left the Forbidden City at the big gate, she turned to me and said: "Mr. Brown, you are an American. True, is it not, your country is *only* two hundred years old?" I was somehow taken aback, embarrassed, and did not respond. I wanted to say—"No, *three* hundred years, going back to the colony, but rejected the thought as absurd in view of the tremendous sweep of China's history where paper was invented 5,000 years ago, about the time China developed a thing called "bureaucracy," a contagion that certainly has come to America.

Anyway, about this time in the 17th Century, the Browns dropped the final "e" in their surname, either out of laziness or dyslexia. There is no record. Sudbury, Massachusetts, Boston, Cambridge, Concord, Lexington were close-knit communities in those days when you could not hold civil or military office unless you were a member of the church, in good standing. The highest rank of government was accorded the town pastor or minister. Morality, law and administration went along together.

When I was six or seven, my father, George Estabrook Brown—searching for gaps in his ancestral tree—
would take me, against my will, to graveyards in these
contiguous neighborhoods of New England. I could never
understand *why* on a nice Saturday I was forced to examine
grey fading gravestones on the gravelly slopes of little
churchyards. My father would tell me that I should cheer
up because we were tracking down together the critical
events of ancestors' lives—*when* they were born, *who* they
married, and *when* they died. During these unhappy visits
to Massachusetts graveyards, I learned firsthand by studying the stones that 17th century men married two, three
and four times, their wives lined up in the grave beside
them, likely their female death coming in childbirth. And
many, many, children. Little gravestones to match the
grave. Some in these early days not living beyond the first
year, beyond the second or third. Children, I came to
understand, were cruelly diminished by diseases now almost forgotten, now controlled and eliminated by the mir-
acles of medicine. Each age has its mysterious burdens.

As a result of perseverance and arcane Sherlock
Holmes deduction, my father was able to establish salient
links of his family between the new world and the old. He
proudly contributed his findings to the American Genealogical Society, which, for five dollars, sent him a certificate of excellence. He had inherited his curiosity about his
ancestors from his own father, John Adams Smith Brown,
who also spent untold avocational hours tracking down his
forebears. Such searching activity, I suspect, is not ac-
quired but is compulsive. You do it surely because you
can't help yourself.

What to remember is that all these ancestors somehow found each other. So the Browns, Estabrooks, Willards, de Rapalyées, etc. became intertwined. I've been

told that propinquity is the great matchmaker. Without such matchmaking, I'm afraid you would not be here. The chance of your even being alive on this earth in this year are oddly 200 billion to one. So count your blessings and struggle on.

I like the story of the Estabrook line. You are in that line since your name at baptism is Julia *Estabrook* Hoyt. Their roots are in Holland (Estaubrugge) as early as 1387. As the twig is bent so grows the tree. There are records of the Estebrok (sic) family in 1413 at Okehampton, County of Devon and diocese of Exeter, England. Many were priests who, the records show, held no land, but willed only personal property divided among family and servants. The pioneer Estabrooks in America were Puritans, a religious group that found themselves at odds with constraints on their worship and beliefs.

In 1660 two Estabrook brothers in their early twenties decided to go to the English colony in America where there was greater freedom to practice one's religion. These adventurers were Joseph and Thomas Estabrook. They had received preparatory education for college in England. Both enrolled in the Class of 1664 at Harvard College, a class numbering no more than 25 students. The main course of study was religion. Today you can scramble to find a class featuring elements of religion, ethics or morality, but remember, this was 324 years ago.

The plot thickens. Another of your ancestors, Simon Willard, also a puritan, had come to Massachusetts earlier for religious freedom in April 1634—thirty years earlier. He settled in Cambridge and took up 100 acres with a house on it, on the Brighton side of the Charles River. He was a merchant who traded with the Indians, with whom he maintained the best relations. He became friends with a leading clergyman of the day, the Reverend Peter Buckley, a man of great eloquence and power. (He is thought to be an ancestor of Judge James Lane Buckley and his journalist brother William F. Buckley, Jr., but the Judge says no.)

On April 2, 1635, a grant was made by the General Court (Colony administration) of a "plantation" at Musketaguid to Peter Buckley, Simon Willard and a dozen others. The settlement was later called Concord. Colony Governor Winthrop immediately sent carpenters to Concord, "to take possession of the place and to raise some buildings." In 1636 Peter Buckley was appointed minister at Concord (there was only one) and remained until 1650 when he was succeeded by his son, Edward Buckley.

Simon Willard participated in the Reverend Buckley's services for years, was elected to the General Court, was appointed a judge for a period of 30 years, was named chief military officer in the country, a position of responsibility in those days when there was always the fear that sleep might be invaded by the sound of the Indian war whoop and the unnerving blow of the tomahawk—or worse—perhaps, the shrieks of wife and children. Incredibly, this concern was ever present. Subsequently Simon Willard sold his property in Concord and bought a farm at Still River, now Harvard College, and after leadership in the King Philip's Indian War (which devastated this New England area), Simon Willard died of influenza in 1676. His second and third wife were sisters of the first President of Harvard College.

Now in 1667 your ancestor Joseph Estabrook, three years out of Harvard, was ordained by the Reverend Edward Buckley, the minister in Concord who had followed his father, Peter Buckley. He became a colleague of Edward

Buckley at the Concord Church and on the Reverend Buckley's death in 1696 Joseph Estabrook was chosen to take his place. He continued in this office until his death on September 16, 1711, at the age of 71 years. Of his death, the Boston News Letter of September 18, 1711 said: "This day was interred in Concord the Reverend Joseph Estabrook, minister in said town for about forty years. He was eminent for his skill in the Hebrew language, and was a most orthodox, learned and worthy divine; of excellent principles in religion, indefatigable laborious in the ministry, and of holy life and conversation."

While living in Concord, Joseph Estabrook was repeatedly urged to leave and go to Boston. They said "he is too bright a star to be muffled up in the woods amongst the savage Indians, and ought to come to Boston where he could do more good." He, however, thought differently and determined to stay in Concord among his "Indians." His salary at the Concord church was 80 pounds a year, of which 40 pounds was paid in money and the balance in grain.

Julia, I like the de Rapalyée family story even better because it's somewhat unexpected and yet at the same time so close to where I've been for 61 years — Manhattan Island, where you were born and live now. The de Rapalyées, to the extent to which we can trace, were part of a religious sect called Huguenots (Protestants) in France. For their spiritual beliefs they were persecuted brutally and cruelly, and in the 17th Century were expelled or forced to flee from France. They became, as many do today, refugees.

In the early 17th Century the point of maximum personal freedom in Europe was Holland. There the

Dutch practiced high tolerance towards the spiritual beliefs of others. Their main interest was in trade. In Holland's harbors the Dutch flag on its vessels showed red and white stripes—emblem, some thought, of freedom and liberty. When America 150 years later adopted its own flag of liberty, the red and white stripes of Holland were intelligently incorporated into its own stars and stripes. I suppose as refugees in Holland there may have been less opportunity for the de Rapalyée family, so the parents of the first European child born in the officially established colony of New Netherland (Manhattan) (Sara de Rapalyée, dutched up as "de Rapalie) took the first boat to the Colony, now New York, in 1625.

This first boatload of settlers sent by the Dutch West India Company on the *Nieuw Nederlandt*, with the masthead of Saint Nicholas on the bow, were not Dutchmen but Protestant Walloons from French Flanders who had fled, under religious persecution, to Leyden.

This new community in the first quarter of the 17th century was known as "New" Amsterdam. It is true that the *real* minority in New York City today are the descendants of the first Europeans who settled here in the early 17th century.

New Amsterdam, like Amsterdam at the time, was a melting pot of people right from the beginning. A dozen languages were spoken in this community. Here lived Scandinavians, Germans, Sephardic Jews (and a synagogue below walled Wall Street) and blacks, both slave and free. Also Italians like Pietro Caesar Albertis and Poles like Albrecht Zabriskie. The de Rapalyées liked where they were and seldom strayed from the environs of Manhattan, Brooklyn and up the Hudson to Albany. When I was a freshman at Yale College, I asked the good-natured maid who cleaned our dormitory what was her name. She said, "My name is Mrs. de Rapalyée."

Once I heard that the Prince of Wales visited Philadelphia in the 1930's for a glorious weekend attending numerous parties along the fabled Main Line. After much entertainment and champagne, a hostess at a final dinner party was startled when the Prince of Wales fixed steady eyes on her and asked earnestly: *"Tell me please, if I may. What is a Biddle?"*

You may ask what is a Megargee—surely the most convoluted, albeit unpretentious name. The history of this tribe is illusive. My father tracked his own family. My mother is Miriam Rossiter Johnson Megargee. So this burden was left to me and I can't say I've been successful. Genealogy is, after all, a curious alchemy of memory, myth and bluff. Sometimes you can get a whiff of what went before, not always. The Megargees came to America in the 18th century when their name was Megargel, which is equally awkward! Sounds more like an over-the-counter drugstore mouthwash.

The early Megargees went straight to Philadelphia, following Quaker William Penn. It has always given me a sense of encouragement to find out that the first Megargees in old Philadelphia were rag pickers, before they discovered, with Parisian chemical techniques of the Benjamin Tilghman family, that rags and a good wash made the finest writing paper in the world. The Megargee Paper Mills produced quality paper for generations, until your great grandfather, Irwin Megargee, died suddenly in the early 1900s leaving no male Megargee in the line to succeed him in the paper business, only four daughters, one of whom, Miriam, my mother, married your grandfather George Estabrook Brown.

Your grandmother, Miriam Megargee Brown, who has gone back to the Philadelphia area to live out her life, told me, after her father's death, she used to have to go to Philadelphia as a child to the law office of her grandfather William Francis Johnson in the first years of this century to show her school report card. She says he was formidable in his flowing white Tolstoyish beard and formal cutaway. He would apply spectacles and "harrumph" a number of times before securing her promise to be more diligent and do better next time.

William Francis Johnson was a good man. I think you would be proud of him too. He graduated from Central High School in the 1850s in Philadelphia. This school then and even today has a reputation for discipline and excellence. Maybe they go together. After graduation he went directly into a law office where he observed, worked and read law. In 1860 he was admitted to the bar of the Commonwealth of Pennsylvania. He practiced as a Counsellor-at-Law half a century. In 1909 he was given a dinner by fellow lawyers and judges to commend him for longevity and service. He was presented with a silver cup to mark the occasion.

His life contained no instant glamour, no high office in government, no written novel to startle the bourgeoisie. He taught law at the University of Pennsylvania without compensation (Contracts, Jurisprudence, Equity and Orphans' Court). He wrote four volumes of law which read pretty true to this day. He served clients everyday and was seen going back and forth to court in a white high hat in the 1890s. When he died in 1910 his desk contained hundreds of legal bills that had been prepared by law clerks but had mercifully never been sent out.

On November 26, 1928, when I was six, my grandfather, John Adams Smith Brown, gathered all his family together for a family reunion in Philadelphia. His father, George Brown, was the first to leave Massachusetts. He settled in Philadelphia, summering in Chelsea, Atlantic City. My grandfather lived in 1928 as a widower at The Wellington Hotel on Rittenhouse Square in Philadelphia. I remember his apartment as smartly done and neat. On his bureau I recall, to my surprise, a framed photograph of his own tombstone with his name cut across it in Renaissance letters, discretely omitting the date of death.

At the family reunion your great-Grandfather, John Adam Smith Brown was 70 years old. He was a tidy if not fastidious man. He loved every moment of life. He adored innocent jokes and was not above making bird sounds and barking dog noises to disconcert haughty people in public places. He was intensely curious and to his last never was afraid to learn something. His book of conclusions was never closed.

This was my first reunion so I was wary of what to expect. His planning of the event at The Wellington put us all at ease. He was the host and acted the part with enthusiasm.

He told us that he was happy to be 70, in good health and to be able to gratify his "great desire" to have a reunion of all his children and grandchildren and to bring them together to "establish in the minds of each of them the memory of having been in the presence of each other . . . "

Then he said something that touches me to this day: "It is difficult," he said, "to easily reconcile the passing of years, that is, when so many at seventy are gone, but to appease this situation it seems 'the Scheme of Life' then automatically asserts itself and *memories* of the incidents of life in general become very apparent, in fact, most of

these memories afford real pleasure when dwelt upon, this
to my mind is as it should be, for as the desires of life and
the former yearnings for achievements so pale as to lose
their glamour then these memories become the substitutes
and are very comforting."
   Then he finished by quoting two lines of advice:
"Slumber not in the tents of your fathers.
The world is advancing, advance with it."

Love
PETER

Carnegie Hill
New York City

−IX−

THE IMPORTANCE OF A TEACHER

Justice Oliver Wendell Holmes, Jr., once said that the life of the law is not logic but experience. My experience is that in any walk of life or career there is nothing more important than a teacher. Teachers and mentors can be found in every area of endeavor. In China the teacher has always been revered. In early America the teacher was honored. Unfortunately, this is less so today and a turnabout in this attitude would be salutary in America, as the subtle effects of a good teacher can be extraordinary.

There is no such thing as a self-made man or self-made woman. If we look back keenly we can all recall the teachers in our lives who have made a difference to us. The first I recall is Miss Perrin when I had to enter the education system by attending a girl's school. I remember the founding headmaster at St. Andrew's School, Walden Pell II. His precepts and example are sterling. Then there was our English teacher at that school in Delaware, John Ellis Large. For four years he took about a dozen rough and insensitive students through the basics of grammar and literature so that when we came to graduation the candles of interest in literature in each of us were lit.

The teacher in my life who encompasses the best qualities of the teaching art is J. Edward Lumbard, a United States Circuit Court Judge in New York City, still active on the Federal bench after over 33 years. In setting forth attributes that make a teacher important, I choose to let Judge Lumbard serve as an example.

Judge Lumbard was born in New York City in 1901, graduated from Harvard (BA 1922, LLB 1925, LLD 1970), was an Assistant United States Attorney under Emory Buckner, became a highly regarded litigator in the federal and state courts, was a senior partner of the distinguished Donovan Leisure firm before accepting appointment in 1951 by President Dwight D. Eisenhower to the office of the United States Attorney in New York. This official position is considered the most important prosecutorial office in America.

Judge Lumbard immediately set about to recruit a team of young assistants, much as Emory Buckner had done before in recruiting him and such persons as John Marshall Harlan. When he had screened and chosen 60 assistant U. S. Attorneys in the new Eisenhower administration, he had the task of personally teaching them what to do, what not to do and how to do it. It was, in retrospect, an enormous task from the beginning and often took all his time around the clock, week after week. Most of his assistants had no experience, certainly no criminal experience, and had to start from scratch.

In 1978 those former assistants who survived gathered at a dinner to pay tribute to their chief on the 25th anniversary of his appointment as United States Attorney.

I remember saying at that dinner, in a chorus of former assistants' toasts, that during our time in that office and for every year since then, for a quarter century, "You have been our teacher." There in the room were the once green and coarse assistants, now transformed, who had been taught by this teacher: eight judges, federal and state, with two candidates for the bench gestating in the wings; nine commissioners; seven professors of law; three United States Attorneys from the Southern District of New York; two law school deans; six Bar Association presidents; two Legal Aid Society presidents; a State Attorney General; an Ambassador; General Counsel of the Army; an Ombudsman of the Railroads; a Deputy New York City Mayor; a State Senator; numerous Assistant Attorneys General; many leaders of the litigation bar and counsel galore to various public bodies.

One veteran pupil of Judge Lumbard, Frederic S. Nathan, wrote each former assistant before the dinner requesting that he or she write a letter to Judge Lumbard, for binding and presentation at the dinner, telling him as explicitly as we could, what his teaching had meant in our professional lives.

My letter, one of many presented by the assistants, is set forth below. As I reread it today, over 10 years later, it expresses as best I can, the appreciation for what Judge Lumbard did for this group of young assistant prosecutors and tries to tell the critical importance of a teacher:

March 8, 1978

Dear Judge Lumbard:

Sometimes when you write a letter to thank someone it is because of a recent hospitality or perhaps a good turn well appreciated. This situation is unique. Here I write to thank you for your exceptional leadership and innumerable kindnesses over a quarter of a century.

On Friday evening, April 7, we will be gathered together to celebrate with you and give thanks on the 25th

Anniversary of your appointment by President Dwight Eisenhower to the significant position of United States Attorney for the Southern District of New York. Your acceptance of this post in the service of the United States was fortunate in many aspects but for your young and green Assistants, employed by you that Spring in 1953, it was a stunning experience.

Through painstaking effort you taught these young lawyers what they know. We will not forget. As Henry Brooks Adams in his "The Education of Henry Adams" observed:

"A teacher affects eternity; he can never tell where his influence stops."

We do not thank you so much for hiring us but rather for teaching us so much that is not written down and for being a true role model all these years and into the future—a continuing source of inspiration.

The great John Bunyan told us long ago:

"You have been so faithful, and so loving to us, you have fought so stoutly for us, you have been so hearty in counselling of us that we shall never forget your favor toward us."

So one can see that the indelible contributions you have made to your young Assistants have not been limited to our service in that great office together but, in addition, to the ensuing years as we struggled to emulate in bits and pieces the basic lessons you gave to us.

In those salad days the United States Attorney's Office had 55 young Assistants under your tutelage, most of whom had just received license to practice. In that office you also took time to train about 45 students in their third year of law school and each summer an additional 45 law students who assisted us in the preparation for trial and sat at the counsel table during trial. One who worked with us is the present United States Attorney, Robert B. Fiske, Jr. Bob Patterson, Julio Nunez and I in early 1953 had been working under Chief Counsel John Marshall Harlan at the New York State Crime Commission. The grapevine gave us the word: Judge J. Edward Lumbard was the choice of President Eisenhower to be the United States Attorney: a well-recognized office for independence and clout. We thought of those who had held that post with distinction: Henry Stimson, Emory Buckner, Thomas Dewey and now, with a dramatic change of Administration, the post was offered to a man described by our boss, Chief Counsel Harlan, as "one of the most able and finest men I have known." To put it mildly, we were anxious to join the Lumbard team in the most important prosecution office in the country. The three of us were interviewed by you and, despite our shortcomings and green youth, were hired to become part of the Lumbard Group. We were on board and there was much to be done.

I remember how thrilled my mother was. She told everyone: "My son is Assistant United States Attorney for the Southern District of New York." One day I explained to her that there were 60 Assistant United States Attorneys in the Southern District of New York. She wept.

People came on board the Lumbard ship that spring, summer and fall at different times and with different experiences but in each case, I believe it is fair to say, with an extraordinary enthusiasm to work and *learn* under the leadership of a man who had already made a deep mark on life as a lawyer, a prosecutor, a constructive-minded community leader and a judge.

What is it then that you have taught us and why is it that we are in your debt for these kernels of truth? There are many things you taught us too numerous to recall. Some came to us from you in the hallways or during recess in Court, perhaps a pithy note passed at counsel's table, a telephone call at night or Sunday afternoon, an oblique remark at a meeting of counsel, those weekly seminars with practical application to the work at hand and at the same time with principles enunciated of general application or just a few words at our gatherings outside the office. All of these inculcating impressions flow back to mind. Some are hard to extricate because over the years we tend to think that we thought of them ourselves.

A Chinese philosopher, Lao Tzu, many centuries ago, wrote a poem about "A Leader" which ends:

"But of a good leader who talks little
When his work his done, his aim fulfilled
They will all say, 'We did this ourselves.'"

Best recollection retrieved reveals some concepts you conveyed to us:

A lawyer has a duty not only to the law and his profession but to public service. You went beyond Elihu Root, Sr., who said to students at the Yale Law School in 1904:

"He is a poor-spirited fellow who conceives that he has no duty but to his clients and sets before himself no object but personal success."

You pointed out the necessity for public service at great sacrifice and, next, public service intertwined with regular professional obligations and finally the real importance of helping other lawyers in their work including enhancement of their careers.

By introducing us to hard work and alternating periods of relaxation together, we all learned the observation of Sir Walter Scott that a barrister, if he has any talents at all, is the best companion in the world. You taught us that the only way to grow in ability was to take chunks of real responsibility at the early stage. Sink or swim. Both are educational. With all the philosophy and pseudo-philosophy in today's world, you gave us to understand the importance of being a believer in people and instead of pontificating about what should be done, you showed us the significance of setting a personal example.

You taught us that leadership necessitated the ability of expressing oneself clearly, accurately, logically and persuasively, the talent to communicate knowledge and ideas. You were not interested in creating 60 specialists but rather *generalists* whose broad skills allowed proficiency in a variety of areas and, where necessary, in coordination with a specialist.

You taught us discipline. *Sine qua non.* Every brief is a labor; every trial a city to be built.

You taught us to grasp the decent opportunity. When a young lawyer hesitated at the offer to join the Lumbard team, you softly pointed out to him that life was akin to a merry-go-round where if, astride your assigned wooden horse, you passed up the gold ring, it may not be there when you come around again.

•   •   •

I can hear the sounds echoing still down the horseshoe corridors of the third and fourth floors of the Federal Courthouse, where we had our office:

"Look here, George Bailey, how many times do I have to tell you: Never assume a goddamn thing." "When you go into Court, there is no substitute for preparation. Know your facts and know your law. You must master your case." "I have spent a lot of time exploring this matter but I tell you you cannot build your case without hard work." "Get in there and grasp the elephant. Advocacy is art."

An Assistant on the 17th floor Court of Appeals was twenty-five minutes into his case when Judge Learned Hand, hand on chin, gazing out the window, loudly asked his two brother judges: "What does the boy want?" You gently reminded us every week to tell the Court the issue and what we want.

And:

"If you want to be a devastating opponent, be conscientious, fair, courteous, articulate and honest."

One day at our weekly seminar you startled us by saying:

"Why, if you are courteous to the Court and fellow counsel, they will think you are a better lawyer than you are."

At regular meetings you introduced outside leaders of the bar who pointed out to us principles you already deemed important for us to know. Once on such an occasion you introduced Learned Hand who immediately thundered at us:

"You young people! You out there. When you come to the Court of Appeals do not be, never be, indignant. [Pause] You may ACT indignant. But never *be* indignant."

We got the point.

You taught us about cross-examination, the great engine of truth. The elusive art of cross-examination, you said, comes to fruition, perhaps, after 5,000 witnesses— each different—each needing a different approach—and most of all, some needing no examination at all.

You insisted on the strength, rather than the weakness, inherent in being respectful and candid with the Court. Unbelievable to us, you would appear in Court when we were trying a case and many times know more about the battle than we did. When the verdict came in, somehow you knew and let us know what you thought about the job performed for the United States—good or bad.

You tried to teach us to be brief. Some of us learned this tenet. Some did not.

You taught us to recognize the shortness of life in advocacy. Go to the jugular. Put that up front! What is it you want to say—then say it. You urged us to desist from walls of words. You detected the passion of many lawyers, some recently out of Dickens' Chancery Court, to trip one another up on slippery precedents and grope knee-deep in technicalities.

When the floodgates of advertising now open, I recall your talk to us one late afternoon to the effect that lawyer advertising was not bad so long as it was invoked legitimately. You suggested that this might be done by trying a case well or writing an excellent brief. You abhorred the sort of lawyer who would obtain an indictment of a narcotics ring and leave behind in the red file jacket a copy of the indictment and a press release with the headline: "Assistant United States Attorney Jones Smashes Narcotics Ring!" and nothing else.

From you we learned about facts—dug out with perseverance and honesty, presented in a way easily grasped:

"Make sure your mind is in gear before you set your mouth in motion."

You raised our sense of pride.

"When you go into Court you are representing this Office. And what's more you are representing the United States. When you are outside this Office, you represent this Office and you are accountable."

You gave us courage. More times than we liked or would admit, we came up against attorneys of long experience who abused the truth, the Court and us into the bargain. You convinced us that the Court had the experience to know how to deal with misleading briefs and deceitful persons. You urged that the integrity of a lawyer in any case is a strong factor in the Court's response.

You taught us to work together, to cooperate in myriad ways with each other, all for a common objective. You have instilled the spirit of cooperation down the years and evidences of this helpfulness among your assistants still remain. As a result, the practice of the law is more rewarding, more interesting and more fun.

Fortified with your lessons and example, the Lumbard Assistants tend to respond quickly to a call for help within and without the profession and when they do they bring with them a variety of principles learned from you, not the least of which are "Don't assume a goddamn thing" and "Thank you for all that you have done for us." We will never forget.

Sincerely
PETER MEGARGEE BROWN

−X−

TIME AND WISDOM

The concept of time is so illusive that philosophers have pondered it and debated about it since the beginning of it.

Theories of explanation have swung from Plato's neat idea of a central big clock in the heavenly sky to Albert Einstein's theory, published in 1915, of the relativity of time in space. We brood over time in less scientific ways—how short is time when we are occupied and happy; how painful and long it is when we are oppressed and suffering like the numbing anxiety of being imprisoned or ill—or a private in the army.

One thing is certain: time for us on earth is finite. There is by fate or divine judgment a certain number of days allotted to us and a lesser number that can be considered healthy, happy and vigorous. From this follows that the most important question affecting us is: How do we intelligently use the time we have left?

In the 1940s, I learned that long ago there was a certain walled garden in Peking, China, near the Forbidden City, that had writing on the wall. The Chinese visitor, sitting placidly in the warmth of the afternoon, was surprised to read in bold yet graceful script, the following message, quite distilled:

"It is later than you think."

Time is precious and little of it left in which to accumulate wisdom. Time precedes wisdom. First time (and experience)—then, only then, wisdom. The people of the East, for some reasons, perhaps culture and patience, are more understanding of the element of time and the subsequent acquisition of wisdom.

Overheard recently was a conversation between two young people riding the New York subway downtown. One said, "Margo, have you read professor Bloom's book, "Closing of the American Mind?" To which Margo replied: "No, I'm graduated from college."

There are indications if not proof that substantial numbers of Americans conceive that their education is complete on receiving a high school certificate or college diploma. In reality, no one really completes an education until the end of his or her time on earth. Justice Holmes read, and was read to, the great classic books, and good contemporary books until he passed away in his nineties. When President Roosevelt paid a courtesy call on the Justice in 1933 he found Holmes in his library reading Plato. "Why are you reading Plato, Mr. Justice," the President inquired. "To improve my mind, Mr. President," Justice Holmes replied.

James A. Farley, the popular political advisor to Franklin D. Roosevelt, once sat next to a Chinese gentleman on the high dais of New York's Waldorf Astoria one evening in long silence through soup, chicken, salad and dessert. Not a word exchanged. Finally, Farley, determined to break the ice, turned to his Chinese neighbor and said,

"Well, Sir, how are things in China?" There was more silence. Then the Chinese gentleman looked searchingly toward Farley and said slowly and precisely: "These last thousand years are not too bad."

We must try, in the haste of our daily travails, to take the time to perceive the longer view—the vision that eludes most of us in this modern world so intent on the short term result and the bottom line.

When our parish was built in 1929 the rector, Henry Darlington, retained a fine lady sculptor, Malvina Hoffman, to design the pulpit and its inscription for the inspiration of the congregation. The rector took the message from the scriptures: "WHERE THERE IS NO VISION, THE PEOPLE PERISH." When the first service took place on Easter Day, 1929, the wardens and vestrymen were distressed. "What is it?," the rector asked. "Well," they said, "the sculptor has done a marvelous job, but she left out of the inscription the word "NO!"

When we are asked why we don't do certain things to improve our minds, hearts or bodies, our usual response is quick—"we don't have time." At least that is my usual response. Time is not a gift allocated only to the rich, the talented and the indolent. It is allocated equally to all—24 hours a day parceled out to each of us. The difference is only *how* we utilize the gift, how we plan and discipline ourselves. Observation and experience show quite clearly that our lives grow sweeter only if we learn to use our time wisely and on a firm pedestal of understanding. The Old Testament book of Leviticus said it succinctly—a direct message to Americans—"With all thy getting, get understanding."

Some concrete suggestions come to mind. So-called vacation reading should be terminated. The books are apt to be light (mindless) or trendy or just trash. If we read 40% trash, it's like snack eating of 40% fat. Both lead to fatter heads, less fun and less wisdom. There is a discipline of learning, a lifetime enterprise. We can get up early and read and write. The newspapers, I think, are *not* unimportant. Read them every day after your stomach is settled. They tell us, graphically, every day, of the disintegration of many areas of our society, the anomie of our precious civilization. If we think of our life as a *whole*, we can, in various ways, often in small ways, make a difference, uplifting the slide here and there, perhaps, together, lifting the social fabric in important areas.

By observation and appreciation alone we can extend all the envelopes of our lives. By selection of high priorities on our time we can be more sensitive to appreciation of the good over the mediocre.

The good of literature, art, health and love can extinguish the fickle and the banal, which cause the most horrible disease of all—ennui. We can try to relate our spirits to higher levels of thought, literature, art and their reflection in our memories. This process can become fresher, more exciting and more enjoyable day to day.

As children, in the hallway of our home, there was a large mahogany grandfather clock, its Trinity and Westminister chimes booming away, night and day. We liked to stand up close and watch the minute hand go "tick-tock, tick-tock," rhythmically, repeatedly. "Tick-tock," doing the same excited jump of a fraction of an inch every second. We were always intrigued to do this close-up observation. We wondered and marvelled at the model of the passage of time. The eerie thing about the grandfather clock (in our house for 71 years), is that the hands always moved in one direction only, never backwards. No frolic and detour. Time moves inexorably forward, and we, whether we like it or not, are carried along with it.

But the carapace of our memory-recall system, properly stimulated, can go backwards, can search out selectively and relive the best of days before yesterday. This method can serve us without expense or indulgence and, assuming we have something lovely to remember, we can catapult our minds and our spirits to higher sunnier grounds. In today's world this can be a blessing.

To the wise there is always enough time. In most cases there is really no good reason to slow down or literally "retire." There are to the optimist and the plucky always new phases of life to live, to enjoy yourself and with others, providing more capital for your energetic memory bank. Always growing, stretching ourselves, never becoming surfeited or set in our ways leading to paralysis of personality. The virtuous man and woman, Aristotle reminded us, is an *active* person.

We sometimes forget that the only purpose of mankind's time marks such as days (24 hours), weeks (7 days), months (28–31 days), years (365 days and leap year for adjustment!), century (100 years, coming up again), is an *artificial* measure for functional convenience. Such markings are otherwise meaningless to the unsuperstitious. The clock and the calendar tell us that time flies. What shall we do with what is left?

To participate in the high enjoyments of pursuing the golden mines of our memory we must start as early as we can to fuel the recollection system and feed it through continuity, observation, story-telling, literature, history and study—all through our lives—which can, in most cases, lead to becoming more wise. We become more content, more enlightened, even more illuminated. One can go so far as to wager that such an individual program of memory storage and liberal use might be deemed the pursuit of happiness that Thomas Jefferson dreamed of to the day he died, just a few hours before the Fourth of July.

Harvard Professor Erik H. Erikson, in the ninth decade of his life, with his partner-wife Joan, tells us, in a recent interview together in Cambridge, that lots of old people don't get wise, "but you don't get wise *unless* you age." He sees in later years the development of human interdependence. "Life doesn't make any sense without interdependence," Mrs. Erikson, also a teacher, said. "We need each other and the sooner we learn that, the better for us all." This kind of homespun wisdom is disarming.

Professor Erikson speaks poignantly of the wane of one's physical and sensory abilities at the end of life's journey. He recognizes that at that final period we consciously reflect back on the course of our lives—comparing our dreams and hopes with the realities of what did happen. He believes this reflection on our memories in later years brings to us the wisdom of humility, a realistic appreciation of one's competence as well as one's limits.

There are more modes of thinking than logic, Professor Erikson insists. Reflections on the complexity of our lives follow new ways of perceiving what our life is about, perceptions that merge logical, sensory and esthetic concepts.

The Eriksons believe that wisdom has little to do with formal education. "What is real wisdom?", Mrs. Erikson asked recently in the interview by Daniel Goleman, published in the *Times*. "[Wisdom] comes from life experiences, well digested. It's not what comes from [only] reading great books. When it comes to understanding life,

experiential learning is the only worthwhile kind; everything else is hearsay."

What the Eriksons seem to be telling us is—live
your life actively and deeply, think on those things that are
lovely, true and of good report, store up your memories in
the banks of your mind (where thieves cannot break
through and steal) and play back your recollections creating a sense of completeness, of personal wholeness, strong
enough to sustain us, in affectionate regard, until the end.

POSTLOGUE

THE POWER OF REMEMBRANCE

Showing a friend the manuscript of this book on a recent summer day, I was urged to read Marcel Proust's continuous novel A *la recherche du temps perdu* (REMEMBRANCE OF THINGS PAST), originally published in eight parts in 1913, 1919 and 1920. My uneven education had not included assignment by the schoolmaster of this lengthy embroidered "fiction-autobiography."

So I was fascinated to find that the brilliant introverted writer, Marcel Proust experienced meticulous colorful slow-motion flights of memory, poignant and insightful, filled with flashback scenes of exquisite detail, remembered as if he were present again in the midst of the sight, sound, touch, taste and smell. A personal ingenious recollection, extraordinarily acute, sensitive and true. Proust, using words, paints vividly with a fine brush. Classic recall.

Seemingly without the conscious effort demanded of lesser beings, Proust could resurrect the past with a dynamic clarity and focus that would be difficult to record even if one had actually been there at the time, writing it down.

Proust was of the personal view that it is a labor in vain to attempt *intellectually* to recapture the past: "all the efforts of our intellect must prove futile," he said. The past is hidden, he believed, somewhere outside the realm, beyond the reach of intellect, in some "material object"—in the *sensation* which that object would give us—often a surprise to us. Whether we come upon this elusive material object depends, he said, on chance.

The most celebrated example Marcel Proust narrates of this journey to the past occurred to him as a sensitive boy at a relative's country house in Combray outside Paris. His family came regularly to visit before Easter each year. One day on his return home on a winter day, his mother, seeing he was cold, offered him some tea. He remembers saying no and then changing his mind. His mother sent for one of "those squat, plump little cakes" now indelibly known as "petites madeleines," shaped as the fluted valve of a scallop shell. Proust raised his lips to a spoonful of tea in which he had soaked a piece of the cake.

Proust then reveals in *Swann's Way*, "No sooner had the warm liquid mixed with the crumbs touched my palate than a shudder ran through me and I stopped, intent on the extraordinary thing that was happening to me. An exquisite pleasure had invaded my senses, something isolated, detached, with no suggestion of its origins. And at once the vicissitudes of life had become indifferent to me, its disasters innocuous, its brevity illusory—this new sensation having had on me the effect which love has of filling me with a precious essence; or rather this essence was not in me, it *was* me. I had ceased now to feel mediocre, contingent, mortal. Whence could it have come to me, this all-powerful joy? I sensed that it was connected with the taste of the tea and the cake, but that it infinitely transcended those savors, could not, indeed, be of the same nature. Whence did it come? What did it mean? How could I seize and apprehend it?"

Subsequently, Proust plumbs the origins of this piercing memory. He suddenly recalls that on Sunday mornings at Combray he would go to his Aunt Leonie's bedroom where she ceremoniously nursed her illusory illnesses. She would give him a little madeleine, dipping it first in his own cup of tea. His Aunt augmented the treat by soaking the madeleine in her "decotion of lime-blossom." This recalled ritual—so simple and so subtle—triggered an explosion of remembrance in his mind that encompassed and released long-forgotten memories of Combray, its parks and water lilies, the people of the village, their conversations, encounters and dwellings, the steepled parish church with its colored windows and tapestries, "town and gardens alike, from my cup of tea!"

In this way Marcel Proust used the prime senses of taste and smell to ignite remembrance of things past. I venture that no one has done so much recollection with such depth and precision. Obviously he took enormous joy and exceptional pleasure from his use of memory to enrich his own life, and, in turn, the appreciation of his readers ever increasing over three quarters of a century. He fashioned memory as a symphony to soothe himself and uplift his spirits.

Proust sums up his memories of his own past, reliving them, savoring them, as if at his command, so disciplined were his penetrating retrieval powers—his own *power of remembrance:*

"But when from a long-distant past nothing subsists, after the people are dead, after things are broken and scattered, taste and smell alone, more fragile but more enduring, more insubstantial, more persistent, more faithful, remain poised a long time, like souls, remembering, waiting, hoping, amid the ruins of all the rest; and bear unflinchingly, in the tiny and almost impalpable drop of their essence, *the vast structure of recollection.*"

•   •   •

REMEMBRANCE OF THINGS PAST

"When to the sessions of sweet silent
thought I summon up remembrance of
things past. . . ." and things <ins>dream of</ins> ~~yet~~ to come

ABOUT THE AUTHOR

PETER MEGARGEE BROWN writes books and essays for pleasure. His book, *The Art of Questioning* (Macmillan 1987) has now been published in paperback by Collier Books. His forthcoming book is *Rascals: The Selling of the Legal Profession*. Mr. Brown lives with his wife, Alexandra Stoddard, an author and designer, in New York City. He practices law with his partner, Whitney North Seymour, Jr., at Brown & Seymour, Counsellors-at-Law.